'During Lent, each one of us sets out on a journey of discovery as we prepare for Holy Week and Easter. This book summons us to reflect on the ways in which Abraham and Sarah's journey intertwines with our own, and is an invitation to engage in a new way with these rich and well-loved stories.'
Paula Gooder, Theologian in Residence for the Bible Society

'It is unusual to focus on an Old Testament figure in Lent, but Christians often think of Lent as a journey, and in this book Abraham's journey has a distinctly Lenten shape. This faithful and flawed character becomes a congenial and challenging guide. Meg Warner gets us to read Scripture with care and helps us to make the connections with our own lives now. For groups and individuals, this is a great Lent book that accompanies us to Easter and the continuing life of discipleship in the risen Christ.'
The Rt Revd Nicholas Holtam, Bishop of Salisbury

'With honesty and compassion, Meg Warner leads the reader through Abraham's story. She interweaves Abraham's journeying with her own and creates a space in which her readers can do the same. Full of accessible scholarly insight and pastoral wisdom, this book will be a valuable, comforting and challenging resource for Christians looking for a fresh perspective on Lenten journeying.'
Jenni Williams, Tutor in Old Testament, Wycliffe Hall, Oxford

'Biography meets Abraham meets Lent. In this highly original, delightfully moving Lent book, Meg Warner connects the narrative of Abraham with the drama of all our lives. Accessible, rich and powerful, this is a Lent book that has the potential to change your life.'
Ian S. Markham, Dean and Professor of Theology and Ethics, Virginia Theological Seminary

Meg Warner is Visiting Lecturer at King's College, London and Reader in the Diocese of London. In her professional work, she seeks to hold together academic theological teaching and research with a more popular teaching and writing ministry. Meg is invited to speak regularly at international Biblical Studies conferences and by dioceses around the Anglican Communion and within the Church of England on topics relating to the Old Testament/Hebrew Bible, with a particular focus on Genesis and the Pentateuch. Prior to her move to London in 2013, Meg taught Law at the University of Western Australia and Biblical Studies at Trinity College Theological School in Melbourne, and worked as Executive and Research Assistant to the Primate of the Anglican Church of Australia.

ABRAHAM

A journey through Lent

Meg Warner

First published in Great Britain in 2015

Society for Promoting Christian Knowledge
36 Causton Street
London SW1P 4ST
www.spck.org.uk

British Library Cataloguing-in-Publication Data
A catalogue record for this book is available from the British Library

ISBN 978–0–281–07489–1
eBook ISBN 978–0–281–07490–7

Typeset by Graphicraft Limited, Hong Kong
First printed in Great Britain by Ashford Colour Press
Subsequently digitally printed in Great Britain

eBook by Graphicraft Limited, Hong Kong

To R. – fellow-traveller, midwife, greatest joy

Contents

Preface and acknowledgements

This book is the fruit of my journey with Abraham over the last decade and a half. Little did I suspect when Susanne Boorer set me an essay topic about Genesis 22 in 1999 that I'd still be working on that essay more than fifteen years later! The Abraham stories have been at the heart of my academic work over that time, but have also increasingly come to shape and undergird my way of living. I'm grateful both to those who've been influential in my academic journey with Abraham, especially Mark Brett and Howard Wallace, and to those who've helped me to see the resonances of Abraham's story in my own, especially Nigel Wright, Ken Parker and Catherine Hicks.

I owe a huge debt of thanks to Leigh Mackay, Morna Sturrock and all of the women and men who have so generously supported the Morna Sturrock Fellowship, of which I was the first beneficiary at Trinity College Theological School, Melbourne, between 2009 and 2011.

Most of this book was written during a three-month stay at Virginia Theological Seminary where I held the position of Trotter Fellow in early 2015. I am extremely grateful to my students there, to Dean and President Ian Markham, Vice-President for Academic Affairs Melody Knowles and librarian-extraordinaire Mitzi Budde.

Thank you to the Faculty and staff of the Department of Theology and Religious Studies at King's College, London, which has become my academic home in London and to Head of Department Paul Joyce.

I am extremely grateful to my commissioning editor at SPCK, Philip Law, who believed in this book and who took a gamble on a new author, and to Juliet Trickey who 'got' what I was setting out to do and who I have to thank for the marvellous cover. Thank you to all of the team at SPCK who have made this process such an easy one.

Finally, heartfelt thanks to my father, John Warner, who instilled in me a love of the stories of the Old Testament from an early age, and my husband, R., who now walks those stories with me and without whom this book could not have been.

Using this book

Each of the six chapters of this book is designed to correspond with a week of Lent. You could simply read the book straight through, but you will probably get most value if you read a single chapter each week during Lent. Each chapter is followed by two sets of questions. For **individual readers** there are questions with a generally personal focus. These questions are designed to stretch you in your personal response to the material presented in the chapter. For those reading the book in **groups** there are questions that are less personal in nature and that address issues of interpretation or practical engagement with the biblical text. Of course, individual readers may choose to read and respond to the questions designed for groups and vice versa. If you are a member of a group your group leader will guide you. You will also find some further recommended reading at the end of the book that will assist you if you want to pursue any of the ideas presented in the book.

1

The call
Genesis 12.1–18

'In which state did you formerly reside?'

It was November 2013 and I was at Melbourne International Airport, preparing to board a flight to Washington, DC, to join my fiancé at a biblical studies conference in the USA. Washington wasn't to be my final destination, however. After the conference the two of us would be flying on to London, where he lived and where I would be making my new home prior to our forthcoming marriage. I had spent weeks packing up all my belongings. Nearly everything I owned had been sold or given away. Now all my worldly possessions (apart from twenty boxes, mostly books, still sitting on a Melbourne dockside awaiting shipping) were in two suitcases and a carry-on. The previous fortnight had been a whirl of farewells and packing. Everything had gone remarkably smoothly, until my very last night when I'd found myself physically ill with apprehension and totally unable to sleep.

So it was that, tired and groggy at eight the next morning, having ticked the box on an Australian customs form that said 'Resident Departing Permanently', I encountered the question, 'In which state did you formerly reside?' The question brought me up with a jolt. Here, for the first time, I was being asked to talk about my home in the past tense. I still had to say farewell at the departures barrier to my friends Davo and Sara who had driven me to the airport in their more or less reliable 1974 Land Rover, but as far as Customs were concerned I had already left Australia.

I was setting out on a very big journey. I was leaving behind my flat, my job, my family, my friends and my country in order to go and build a new life in the United Kingdom. Washington was just a convenient stopping point for a few days – a chance to get my breath back, to re-calibrate before setting out on the final leg. The real destination was London, where I would have my first experience of marriage and hopefully find work and friends.

In our biblical story for this first week of Lent we meet Abraham, a Babylonian septuagenarian, who is also setting out on a very big journey. Genesis 12 tells us that Abraham was called by God to leave his country, his family and his father's household and travel to a new country that God would show him. Abraham wasn't alone; he was accompanied by his wife Sarah, his nephew Lot and some servants. It is worth noting that Abraham is called 'Abram' at this point in the story, and his wife 'Sarai'. Later on God will give them their new names, so that eventually they will have left not only country, family and household but even their names (and therefore identities) behind!

Your Lent journey

We'll return to Abraham in a moment, but it is important to remind ourselves that the beginning of Lent is also the start of a journey. If your intention is to read this book through Lent, then you are embarking on a journey and taking the first steps towards a new place that God will show you. You may be reading with a group, or you might be reading alone. Either way, you should be prepared to make a journey. It is unlikely that you will find yourself, like Abraham and me, leaving your country and family to travel physically to a new place, but I can't guarantee it won't happen! But even if your journey isn't the sort that requires suitcases, it is a journey you are setting out on, nonetheless. Who knows where you will be when Easter comes?

This book will be a guide for the journey. For each week of Lent there will be a chapter of this book to read, and some verses from the book of Genesis. At the end of each chapter you will find some questions to help you to think about what you have read.

You may be new to the journey of Lent, or you may have travelled it many times. Either way, it is possible that Abraham will be a new guide for you. Typically, Lent books tend to concentrate on the Gospels, and especially the Passion narratives. Perhaps it may seem odd to you to spend Lent with Old Testament stories. I can guarantee that you will discover that Abraham's story has a distinctly Lenten shape. There are many points at which Abraham's story resonates strongly with the New Testament, and where that happens I will let you know. I hope that you will find that Abraham is a congenial, if challenging, guide and that his story leads you into many of the places you would expect to travel (and some you would not) were you to follow Jesus' path to Golgotha this Lent. In this book you will be offered the chance to learn a little more about the Old Testament, and about Genesis in particular. My primary aim, however, is to help you reflect on the ways in which Abraham's story resembles, resonates with or challenges your own. I will tell you some of my story as we go, in the hope that that will help you to reflect on yours and on how Abraham can be a fellow-traveller with you.

Setting out

Now the LORD said to Abram, 'Go from your country and your kindred and your father's house to the land that I will show you.

> I will make of you a great nation, and I will bless you, and make your name great, so that you will be a blessing. I will bless those who bless you, and the one who curses you I will curse; and in you all the families of the earth shall be blessed.'

(Gen. 12.1–3)

Our text this week is Genesis 12 and the well-known story of Abram/Abraham's call. You have probably heard many times about Abraham's extraordinary trust and how he left his home to travel to a place he'd never been to, at the request of a God he'd never before encountered. You may be thinking that you could never match that kind of faith, or that Abraham's call sounds like one you could never imagine receiving in your busy, twenty-first-century life. How would you even recognize such a call?

Let's look a little more closely at the story. I wonder whether you have ever noticed: when, in Genesis 12.1, God calls Abraham to leave his country, kin and father's house, Abraham has already left! In order to see this, we need to read back a little. We first hear about Abraham and his family at the end of Genesis 11. In v. 31 Terah, Abraham's father, takes Abraham and Sarah and their nephew Lot and leaves their home in 'Ur of the Chaldeans' (in modern-day Iraq) to go to the land of Canaan. This happens before God calls to Abraham! Halfway through their journey, however, the family reaches Haran and settles there. It is a little like my journey to London that had a halfway stop in Washington (except that Abraham probably didn't have to read a conference paper!). The difference is that Terah and his family stay in Haran and never finish their journey. Why not? There are many things that we are never told. We don't know why Terah wanted to leave Ur, why he wanted to go to Canaan or why he decided to stop and settle in Haran. The text tells us that Terah died in Haran

(Genesis 11.32), so perhaps Terah's health was the reason for staying.

It is only at this point that God's call to Abraham comes. Abraham's call, then, is not a call to leave his first home, but to leave the halfway place where he and his family had settled. This doesn't take anything away from the fact that Abraham was called by God, but it does make a difference to how we might understand his call. We can now see in it a mix of human plans and God's plans. Ironically, God is calling Abraham to do exactly the thing that Abraham had already set out to do before he got side-tracked! Once God calls Abraham, however, the journey to Canaan takes on a whole new significance. Canaan is no longer simply a destination that Terah chose and failed to reach. Canaan becomes the destination that God has chosen for Abraham, *and* Abraham becomes the person whom God has chosen for Canaan.

This gives us a new way of thinking about Abraham's call. And it helps us, I believe, in thinking about discerning our own calls. If we are waiting, literally, for a bolt out of the blue to tell us to 'go' or 'do' or 'be', we may find ourselves disappointed or confused. I suspect that for most ordinary people, like Abraham and like me, God's call can be discerned only in the context of a sort of confused mess of our own plans and those of God for us. Each time I have found myself trying to discern a call from God, I have tried to tease out strands of my own desires or frustrations from other strands of what might be God speaking to me. Inevitably, I eventually give up and realize that the two cannot be neatly separated. The two wills, mine and God's, are inextricably bound. Even though I want to know that the 'urge' or 'push' I am experiencing towards some new direction is from God, I need to acknowledge that some of it also belongs to me. This does not mean, of course, that some of it isn't from God too! As a result, it is extremely important that I get as much clarity as I can about my own desires, fears or unacknowledged agendas, in order to work out whether the 'urge' I feel is simple self-seeking. I may not be able to discern clearly which desires are mine and which are God's for me, but it is important to do my best. A spiritual 'director' or 'guide', my parish priest or just a wise friend can be a vital sounding-board in this regard.

Another thing that I generally realize, on each of these occasions, is something that you might also find. You may realize that you are already somewhere along the way to the place where God is calling you. You have already started out. Perhaps you've not got very far. Perhaps, like Abraham, you may have become side-tracked, so that you have 'settled' prematurely in your own version of Haran. Perhaps you've even started to run in the opposite direction – like Jonah setting out for Tarshish (in the far west) when he'd been called to go to Nineveh (in the far east)!

At the beginning of each new Lent we are challenged to discern where it might be that God is calling us. There may be a major piece of discernment that you are currently engaged in, or it may be a smaller-scale (but no less real) discernment about where God wants you to 'travel' over Lent. One of the things that you share with Abraham in this regard is that *you have already set out.* Whether or not you know it, the fact that you have begun to read this book shows that you have already left Ur. You might not have travelled very far, or you might be well on your way to Canaan. You might have got part way to Haran and decided that it would be safer/easier/more comfortable just to stay there. This will be part of your discernment. If, indeed, you find that you have become marooned in Haran, part of your discernment will involve working out exactly what it is that Haran represents for you, and whether you want to stay there.

'I want to be a priest!'

When I flew out of Melbourne for London in 2013 I did have a sense that I was responding to a call. But it is also true that I'd first travelled *to* Melbourne (from Perth, in Western Australia) in order to pursue a call many years earlier. I had given up a lucrative and secure job teaching law at the University of Western Australia and begun theological studies. Even though my parents had viewed this development with some dismay I discovered that I loved the study of theology, and over the first year or two a suspicion that I might be called to ordination as a priest began to grow. I also became aware that I *wanted* to be ordained rather badly. I talked to everybody I could. Some people, including my spiritual director, were dubious. Others encouraged me. I explored every 'lead' to try and get a sense of this vocation, and while some seemed to suggest I might be on the right track, other leads proved to be dead ends.

I had a particular problem in all of this, and it related to my parents. My father is an Anglican priest and he and my mother had only recently returned to my city after having served in a parish on the other side of the country for several years. I adored my parents and it was wonderful to have them back, but it didn't take too long before I began to realize that I had become used to their being away. My faith had altered in that time and I had got used to being the only 'Warner' in the diocese! I didn't know whether I could cope with ordination training in a city where my dad had been such a presence. So I hit on the idea of seeking ordination in the Diocese of Melbourne (which just happened to be on the opposite side of the country). My parents were devastated, but I was determined. So I left. I moved to Melbourne, resumed my theological studies and applied to be ordained.

Six months later I had to acknowledge that in some respects, at least, I had been wrong. Although my study was going well, my health wasn't good, I had got myself into a sticky relationship and I no longer felt a sense of a call to ordination. I pulled out of the ordination process before the church had had a chance to test my vocation. In that latter decision, at least, I knew I'd acted wisely. Both the desire to be ordained and the sense of call to ordained ministry had gone and they've never returned.

Looking back on it now I am in a better position to reflect on the call and my discernment of it. In one sense I could understand my move to Melbourne as having been entirely motivated by my own desires. It had turned out that I hadn't been called to ordained ministry after all, and I had caused a great deal of pain for my parents. On the other hand, I *don't* think that it would be right to say that the move to Melbourne had all just been about me. God had been part of it too, and I *was* responding to a call. It just wasn't a call to ordained ministry. In the longer term the move to Melbourne proved to have been an extremely positive one for me. I had all the resources there that I needed to explore and discern my true calling, *and* I had a chance to build a new, more adult relationship with my parents.

The process of discernment and response to God's call is not an easy one. As a wise spiritual friend of mine used to say, 'You don't get a fax from heaven.' God speaks to us through the circumstances of our lives *and* through our own cares and passions. We see God's will in actions, events and coincidences that could be explained just as effectively in perfectly ordinary everyday terms. It takes some careful attention, and a dash of confidence in ourselves and in God, to see it.

Frequently, like me, you will set out in a direction that you later discern not to have been the one towards which God was leading you. You shouldn't become too dispirited about this – it is just one more challenge for God to work with. The important thing is that you are moving. Discerning God's call can be likened to sailing. You can only travel with the wind, and sometimes the only way to get back to the beach may be to point your stern into the wind, *even if that means heading directly out to sea for a while.* That may be a frightening thing to do, but it may be your only option. Once you have some movement, even if it is not in a direction you eventually want to go, you will be in a position to catch a breeze, trim your sails and head towards your final destination.

If you are already moving, on the other hand – being blown in a positive direction – and you are sailing along without a sense of a need for change, then there is no reason to be wondering whether you should be changing direction. It is the same with discernment. If you are travelling well in your job, family life, prayer life, etc., and you find yourself attracted to some other sort of life, then there is a good chance that what you are experiencing is just your own desire. If God wants you to change direction at that point he will certainly find a way to let you know. You should carry on until you feel that you are being hit over the head with God's new plan for you!

If, on the other hand, you are becalmed, so that you can't feel a hint of a breeze and you feel yourself going nowhere, then it will be up to you to initiate some movement. It doesn't matter too much if it later proves to have been in the 'wrong' direction. The momentum that you build will enable you to catch the next gust and re-calibrate. In sailing, you rarely get to sail *directly* towards your goal. You are more likely to sail off to one side, then return almost to where you set out from, then return to the original direction. Over time this side-to-side progress gets you to your destination. Looking back, you can't see a direct line of travel, but you have arrived nevertheless. Discernment of call can be a lot like this. Looking back you may see a lot of travel from side to side (and some that even looks to be going backwards). You are also likely to see the gifts you received along the way of each of your 'diversions,' *and* how these gifts are now woven into the fabric of your eventual vocation. For example, I might be tempted to think that all those years studying, practising and teaching law had been wasted. In fact, nothing could be further from the truth, and in my theological work I draw on my legal skills constantly. God works with our initiatives and weaves them into a tapestry that is richer than any we could have woven all on our own. In the economy of God, nothing is lost.

Why Abraham?

It is time to get back to Abraham! God's first communication with Abraham, in Genesis 12.1–3, combines a directive ('Go . . .') with several promises. God promises to make Abraham a great nation, to bless him and to make his name great so that he will be a blessing. God tells Abraham that he will bless whomever Abraham blesses and curse whomever Abraham curses. All the families of the world will be blessed in (or through) Abraham. All of these promises appear to come out of the blue, leading us to ask: why Abraham?

At the beginning of Genesis 12 we know only a very limited amount about Abraham. He comes from a city in Mesopotamia and has a wife who is barren and two brothers, one of whom has died. Genesis tells us that by the time Abraham leaves Haran he is 75 years old! The book of Joshua (24.2) tells us that when Abraham's family lived in Haran they 'served other gods', but Genesis itself doesn't say anything along these lines. Really, we don't know anything about Abraham at all that might explain God's choice of him. In one sense the only thing we know about Abraham is something that flows from our previous discussion, and that is that *he had set out*. His father and brother had died, and a second brother seems not to have left Ur. But Abraham was on his way. Is it really as simple as that?

If we know very little about Abraham prior to his call, what do we learn about him afterwards? Certainly we learn something, but the picture is a little mixed. The first thing we notice about Abraham is his obedience. He 'goes', just as God asks. He takes his wife and nephew and all their possessions and household, and sets out for Canaan. When Abraham arrives in Canaan God appears to him again and makes a further promise – this time that he will give 'this land' to Abraham's offspring. Abraham begins to move through the land, beginning in Shechem in the north and moving down through the land towards the Negeb Desert in the south. At significant points Abraham pauses to build altars and to call on the name of God. This appears to be a faithful response to a God whom Abraham has only just met. It is interesting to note, however, that the first of Abraham's altars is built next to a tree, something that Deuteronomy 16.21 later says that God hates!

Abraham's movement through the land is a kind of exploration of it. In a sense Abraham is writing a 'certificate of title' to the land that God has just promised to give to his offspring. The text mentions that there were at that time other people, the Canaanites, already living in the land. This reference to the Canaanites is very casual, like a kind of throwaway line. Nothing is said, for example, about how the presence of the Canaanites and God's gift of the land are likely to impact on one another. It is significant that Abraham is given no instruction to slaughter the Canaanites or to remove them from the land, as the Israelites under Moses and then under Joshua are told to do at a later time (e.g. Deuteronomy 7.2; Joshua 11.20). As we will see in the following chapters, the stories about Abraham in Genesis paint a very different picture of the relationship between 'locals' and 'foreigners' (generally much more peaceful) from that found elsewhere in the Pentateuch (the first five books of the Bible) and in Joshua. We will explore this in Chapter 6.

After moving through the land and building altars and calling on God's name, Abraham does something surprising. He keeps going! He passes all the way through the land until he gets as far as Egypt. Having just been told to go to Canaan and promised that Canaan would be given to his children, the first thing Abraham does is to leave Canaan and go to Egypt! The text tells us that he did this because there was a famine in Canaan. During the biblical period Egypt, with its relatively efficient bureaucratic planning for times of drought, was often a fallback option for those who were unable to feed themselves adequately during drought in Canaan. Egypt's plentiful water supplies and verdant soils meant that even when other countries were in drought food was plentiful in Egypt. Abraham apparently doesn't believe that God's blessings will be enough to help him feed his family, and so he leaves Canaan and goes to Egypt.

Once in Egypt Abraham gets worried. He reasons that as Sarah is a beautiful woman (despite the fact that she must be quite advanced in age) his own life is in danger. Some amorous Egyptian might try to kill him to get him out of the way. As a solution, he asks Sarah to lie and to say that he is her brother rather than her husband. Abraham does not seem at all concerned that this tactic may place Sarah in danger instead of himself! In the event, Abraham proves to have been prescient, if not exactly gentlemanly. The Egyptians consider Sarah very beautiful. They praise her beauty to Pharaoh and Sarah is taken into Pharaoh's house. Things turn out well for Abraham; he is rewarded with lavish gifts from Pharaoh. Things do not, however, go well for the Egyptians. God afflicts them with great plagues, so that Pharaoh calls Abraham, learns the truth about his marriage to Sarah and sends him away, together with Sarah and all their possessions.

Extraordinarily, this story is told not just once but three times in Genesis! Abraham emerges wealthier but not wiser – he repeats precisely the same strategy again in Genesis 20, and Isaac follows suit in Genesis 26. Afterwards Abraham returns from Egypt to Canaan, where he retraces his steps and comes to one of the places where he had built an altar. Here he calls on the name of God once again (Genesis 13.3–4).

You might agree with me that Abraham doesn't emerge from this story covered in glory. He displays concern only for his own well-being – not for that of Sarah or the Egyptians. In what sense, we wonder, is this Abraham to be a blessing? Will all the families of the earth really be blessed in or through him? Egypt was not blessed, but plagued! The story functions, here in its first version, as a kind of inverted mini-Exodus. Israel (as represented by Abraham) goes down to Egypt and attracts the interest of Pharaoh. God sends plagues upon the Egyptians and Israel flees, bearing newly acquired wealth. The primary difference is that in this story the real oppressor is Abraham and not Pharaoh.

What are we to make of Abraham, and why might God have picked him to be the father of his chosen nation Israel? Abraham is neither all good nor all bad. When God asks him to go he simply packs up and goes! Once in the land he demonstrates a certain amount of piety. It is arguable, however, that his piety does not translate into trust – despite God's many promises he apparently abandons Canaan at the first sign of trouble and demonstrates a worrying lack of care for those around him.

Abraham, then, at least at the outset, is no towering exemplar of the faith. It is apparently not for any particular virtue or merit that God chooses him. This is an interesting aspect of the story for us to ponder. Abraham's experience in Genesis 12 suggests to us that God may not choose people on the basis of their particular talents or personal strengths. As we'll see later in this book Abraham develops new skills and sensitivities over time, especially when it comes to dealing with the peoples of other nations, but he doesn't have these at the start.

Personally, I find this rather reassuring. I like the idea that Abraham may not be an exemplar that I have to live up to. Instead, he's someone not unlike me – someone who does well in some respects and in other respects totally messes up. This makes him real in a way that he might not be if he were an entirely admirable character right from the beginning. Because he's real I find that he is someone to whom I can relate and with whom I can sympathize. In short, he is of far greater value to me as a flawed character than he would be as a two-dimensional poster-boy.

People have looked to Abraham to be a model of some sort or another over many centuries. You are probably familiar with the way that Abraham is presented in the Pauline letters, for example (see in particular Romans 4 and Galatians 3). Today members of all three 'faiths of the book' (Judaism, Christianity and Islam) look to Abraham as a common ancestor (through Isaac for Jews and Christians and through Ishmael for Muslims) and therefore as a beacon of hope for multi-faith friendship and reconciliation. We will explore this dimension of Abraham's legacy in Chapter 4.

It appears that Abraham also functioned as a model for Israelites in the later biblical period, and the depiction of Abraham in Genesis almost certainly reflects this. Abraham was an important figure and model, for example, for the Israelites who returned from exile in Babylon in the late sixth century BCE ('BCE' stands for 'before the Common Era'. It is shorthand used by scholars instead of 'BC', which stands for 'before Christ'.) After Jerusalem was destroyed by the Babylonians in 587 BCE many of the Judeans were taken into exile in Babylon. They were allowed to return only fifty years later when the Persians defeated the Babylonians and Persia's King Cyrus allowed Babylon's captured exiles to return to their homelands. If you were to look at a map of the route taken by the Judeans returning to Canaan from Babylon, you would see that it is essentially the same as the route taken by Abraham, from Ur and via Haran.

Many (if not most) Genesis scholars believe that our text for this week, Genesis (11 and) 12, was edited during the period of Persian occupation of Judah that followed (from the late sixth to the late fourth century BCE) so as to depict Abraham as having travelled to Canaan from Babylon, *just as the exiles had*. When the exiles arrived back in Judah they discovered that other Judeans (mostly lower-class artisans), who had not been taken into exile, had taken over the homes, businesses and agriculture of the exiles. It appears that a bitter identity-battle ensued, in which the exiles and those who'd remained competed to be recognized as the 'true Israelites', and that Abraham was claimed by both groups as a legitimating ancestor. Before this editing of the text, Genesis 11 and 12 would have said nothing about Abraham's origins in Ur (or even Haran) so that Abraham was presented as local to Canaan, like those who'd not been taken into exile. His story probably began with his moving around Canaan in Genesis 12.6. In this version Abraham was a 'father' who could be claimed as ancestor by those who'd remained in support of their claim to land and the identity of the true Judeans (see Ezekiel 33.24 as an example). The returners, who wanted to claim Abraham as *their* ancestor, added the tradition that Abraham had originally come to Canaan from Babylon, just as they had, so that they were therefore the true ancestors of Abraham and beneficiaries of the land promise.

Over the next weeks of Lent, as we make our way through this book, we will continue to read the Abraham stories in the context of the events of the fifth century and the Persian occupation of Judah. This will help us to get a picture of the historical background of the Abraham stories, so that we can understand the stories better. We will discover that all sorts of details become clearer, and make more sense, when understood against this background.

But let us, for a moment, come back to thinking about Abraham as a model for us in our time. There are two further things that reassure me about Abraham. These are things that become apparent only as his story continues. The first is that although Abraham continues to make a mess of things sometimes, he learns and grows. In a sense he *becomes* the person God chose. The second, and more important, thing is that God remains faithful to Abraham through everything. God does not abandon Abraham when Abraham gets it wrong – he remains Abraham's God regardless of Abraham's record. Here, of course, is the real point of Abraham's story for us. If we are God's chosen people, and Christians believe that we are all God's chosen people through Christ, then God will be faithful to us, even when we fall short of the mark, as Abraham did and as each one of us does, over and over again.

On the journey

Before I knew it I was through Customs (leaving Davo and Sara to brave the journey home in their Land Rover) and on my way to the departure lounge. I had left Australia and my big journey was finally beginning.

Our Lenten journey, too, has begun. In this first chapter we've seen the importance of 'setting out'. We've met Abraham and followed his 'setting out'. We saw that Abraham's departure from his homeland actually happened long before he became aware of God's special plans for him. Something had happened, however, to cause Abraham's family to abandon their goal of Canaan and settle in Haran. It was in Haran that God met Abraham and called him to Canaan. A careful reading of Genesis 12 (and the end of Genesis 11) has not revealed any clear reason why

God chose Abraham and not somebody else. At the beginning of Genesis 12 Abraham appears to have no special attributes that merit his selection, and by the end of the chapter we are aware that his is a faithful but flawed character. By the end of Abraham's life, I've suggested, we learn that God remains faithful to Abraham despite his various adventures.

I've suggested, too, that you have also 'set out' on your Lenten journey. Your particular journey may not be one that will involve geographical movement. This is a journey that you can take in a single country, a single city, a single room. But it is a journey nonetheless and you should expect things to be different when you reach Easter. I hope this is something that fills you with a positive sense of anticipation! I can't guarantee that the journey will be easy. It may, like Abraham's journey, prove to be perilous. Some difficulties may even arise quite early, and next week we'll focus on some of the particular perils of 'week two'. There are two guarantees that I am able to make, however. The first is that so long as you remain on the journey, you will arrive at your destination. When I say 'your' destination, of course, I don't necessarily mean the one you currently have in mind! 'Your' destination may prove to be somewhere quite different, as I found when I travelled to Melbourne to pursue one vocation and found another. The second guarantee I can give you is that God will be travelling with you. How can I know, you wonder? That is what next week's chapter is all about.

Questions for reflection

For individuals

1 Do you have a sense of having already 'set out' on a journey? If so, did you set out on purpose, or did you only later become aware that you'd set out? If the latter, what were the clues?

2 Where do you think you might be headed? What emotions accompany your answer?

3 Have the Lent and Easter seasons been times of journeying for you in the past? Could you write the story of a Lenten/ Easter journey you've taken?

For groups

1 What expectations do you bring with you to Lent and Easter? How have your previous experiences helped to shape these expectations?

2 What 'new' things did you learn about Abraham in this chapter? What questions do they raise for you?

3 In the past, how have you gone about 'discerning' God's call and God's will for you? Do you have stories or tips to share with the group?

2

The promise
Genesis 15

After these things the word of the LORD came to Abram in a vision, 'Do not be afraid, Abram, I am your shield; your reward shall be very great.' But Abram said, 'O Lord GOD, what will you give me, for I continue childless, and the heir of my house is Eliezer of Damascus?' And Abram said, 'You have given me no offspring, and so a slave born in my house is to be my heir.' But the word of the LORD came to him, 'This man shall not be your heir; no one but your very own issue shall be your heir.' He brought him outside and said, 'Look towards heaven and count the stars, if you are able to count them.' Then he said to him, 'So shall your descendants be.' And he believed the LORD; and the LORD reckoned it to him as righteousness.   (Gen. 15.1–6)

The 'week two' syndrome

When we left Abraham at the end of the last chapter he had embarked on his long journey, leaving his home and bringing his family to the land that God had shown him. We have also embarked on a long journey – a 40-day journey to Holy Week and Easter. You may be beginning to realize just how long this journey of Lent really is! Often it is at the beginning of week two that the sugar cravings really begin to kick in, or the need for a gin and tonic starts to feel overwhelming. Whatever your

Lenten discipline, this is the point when the initial enthusiasm for self-deprivation can start to wane as you realize that there is still an awful lot of Lent to go.

At the same time, you may find yourself beginning to have some questions or doubts. Certainly, you may wonder whether you are going to have the strength and application to keep up your discipline, but you might also begin to question the point of having a Lenten discipline at all. It is not unusual at this point to experience some doubts about your faith. You might wonder what your faith is worth if you are finding it difficult just to go for a couple of weeks without chocolate digestives! On the other hand, you might find yourself ruminating on God's part in all of this. Is God really travelling this journey with you, and will God be there at the end? Perhaps you will experience a fear that Easter, when it finally comes, will be a disappointment, bringing with it no strong sense of new life. You might begin to wonder whether God's promises can be relied on and whether this journey really has a point.

This seems also to be the place in the journey where Abraham (who is still called Abram at this point – see Chapter 1, p. 2) finds himself in this week's reading from Genesis 15. At the beginning of the chapter Abraham has a problem that is causing him to doubt God's promises. We saw last week that God had made several promises to Abraham, including promises of descendants and land (Genesis 12.1–3, 7; 13.14–17). Abraham's problem is that he doesn't have a son and can't see any way of getting one. He is old and Sarah is barren. How could God give him many descendants, and give the land to them, if he doesn't have even one? Just how trustworthy is this God if even the prerequisites don't seem to be being taken care of?

Before we start to look more closely at Abraham's predicament and God's response, let's stay with ourselves for just a bit. The kind of flagging energy, or niggling doubts, to which we can be prone in week two of Lent can, of course, arise at many other times also. In particular, they can occur at times when it seems to us that God hasn't taken care of the prerequisites. If the things we really need don't seem to be available to us it can be very hard to believe that God really has us in his sights. This can be particularly difficult if we think that God has a calling for us, but, like Abraham, we feel that an important resource is missing. For example, you might feel a calling to lay ministry but worry that you won't be able to cope with the necessary study, or that your finances won't stretch to cover it. Alternatively, you might feel called to ordained ministry, but worry about the impact of your ordination on the other members of your family.

I had this kind of problem some years ago. I felt pretty sure that God was calling me to some kind of teaching ministry, but I didn't feel that I was well enough to embark on it. I had been living with ME (or chronic fatigue syndrome) for many years and seemed completely unable to shake it. The amount of activity that I was able to engage in in a day, or week or month, was extremely limited. I would exhaust myself trying and eventually have to admit defeat and go back to bed. This had been going on for years. It seemed cruel of God to give me a calling but not the energy I needed to pursue it. I was in the position of Abraham, who had been promised a future by God but who lacked the resources to live it, and whose confidence, in himself and in God, had taken a hit.

Abraham the champion of faith

You might be beginning to wonder why it is that I am talking about Abraham and doubt, and especially in the context of Genesis 15. This chapter is, after all, the one most closely associated in the minds of Christians with Abraham's faith. In particular, you will probably be familiar with the final verse in the extract from Genesis 15 at the beginning of this chapter: 'And he believed the LORD; and the LORD reckoned it to him as righteousness.'

Christians tend to think of Abraham as something of a champion of faith – a man who is exemplified by his extraordinary faith in God. This Christian tradition about Abraham is due in large part to the interpretation of Evangelical and Reformed churches (including especially the Lutheran Church) of the writings of Paul, especially in Romans 4 and Galatians 3. For Paul, according to this interpretation, Genesis 15.6 expresses something of the very essence of Abraham, and also of the very essence of the idea of justification by faith. The true descendants of Abraham, and the truly righteous, according to this tradition, are those who believe what they have been taught, and not those who are focused on keeping the law or on attaining righteousness for themselves through their own deeds. Not all Christian traditions have interpreted Paul in this way, and in recent years New Testament scholars have been debating 'new perspectives' on how best to interpret Paul's presentation of Abraham. We don't have room to follow all those debates here, but what we can do is to focus on Genesis 15 to see whether the highly influential tradition of Abraham as a champion of faith is really supported there.

I wonder how helpful you have found this Christian presentation of Abraham. If you are a person to whom belief comes easily, then this Pauline model of the believing Abraham may be a great encouragement and a confirmation of your sure faith. If you are not one of those blessed people, you might find the traditional Pauline Abraham more difficult. For example, if you find yourself in a 'week two' place of doubt and uncertainty, how helpful do you find it to be told simply to have faith and to believe? Similarly, how helpful is it to be encouraged to 'be like

Abraham' if you have in the past experienced deception or betrayal at the hands of people you believed or trusted? Surely, under such circumstances a little circumspection is a good thing?

You will notice that the title of this chapter, 'The promise', suggests a focus that is more on God's promise than on Abraham's response of belief. Genesis 15 itself shares that focus. Genesis 15, we will discover, is really more about God than it is about Abraham, and more about God's faithfulness than it is about Abraham's faith. Let's catch up on what has happened to Abraham since the end of last week's story before we begin to explore Genesis 15 itself.

On the road

We saw in the previous chapter how Abraham left his country and his family home and set out for a new country on the strength of God's promises. The intervening chapters of Genesis depict the first steps of Abraham's journey upon entering his new land. In Genesis 12–13 Abraham moves through the land, building altars to worship God but also creating a kind of certificate of title to the land through which he travels; 'Rise up, walk through the length and the breadth of the land, for I will give it to you' (Genesis 13.17). When famine strikes, Abraham travels south to Egypt, endangering both himself and Sarah. God is with them, however, and they return, with Pharaoh's gifts of livestock and slaves, to Canaan where they become 'very rich'. This wealth has implications, one of which is that Abraham and Lot find themselves too wealthy to inhabit the same land. They separate, Lot taking the well-watered plain of the Jordan and Abraham the land of Canaan, which God had promised to him. A rather strange adventure ensues, in which Abraham finds himself to be not just a wealthy grazier but the leader of an army! He leads his servants into battle against the soldiers of neighbouring kings, rescuing Lot and his people and possessions, and receiving a blessing from the priest-king Melchizedek.

In Genesis 15 all of this frenzied activity suddenly stops and Abraham has time to think. This is the point at which Abraham's concerns about his lack of a son and heir start to take hold. When he and Sarah set out from Ur the problem perhaps hadn't seemed insurmountable because Lot, Abraham's nephew, had travelled with them. He could have been an acceptable heir. However, the separation between them has disqualified Lot from this role, and now Abraham is worried that his heir will be 'Eliezer of Damascus' (15.2) or a slave born in Abraham's house (15.3). (Incidentally, scholars have no clear idea who this Eliezer might have been, how he might relate to the slave mentioned in verse 3, or anything else about him at all.) Having an heir was vital in the Canaan of Abraham's time. It was through descendants that a man made his mark on the world, and God's promise, in Genesis 12, to make Abraham a 'great nation' reflects this reality. In Abraham's case, as we've already seen, the problem was particularly acute because all of God's promises to Abraham were dependent on him having offspring. How could Abraham become a great nation if he didn't have so much as a son? What good is a great name without a son to pass it on to? And what is the point of God's promise to give the land of Canaan to Abraham's offspring if Abraham doesn't have any? You can see his problem!

The historical background

Abraham's experience resonated with that of the Judah and Judeans of the fifth century BCE. We saw in Chapter 1 that Abraham's story was probably edited in the years after Judah's return from exile in Babylon in order to reflect something of Judah's own situation and concerns. Post-exilic Judeans were able to see in Abraham's adventures and dilemmas their own experience, and the biblical editors wrote with this in mind.

On one level, things should have been great for the returning Judeans. They had finally been granted the opportunity to return home, for which they had been waiting, and praying for decades. The reality they encountered on their return, however, was not as they had imagined it. The monarchy and the Temple had gone. There was no Israelite king or centralized worship place, and Judah was under Persian occupation. Although the returnees had tended to assume that they would simply be able to return to their own homes and businesses to pick up where they had left off, they discovered instead that their homes and businesses had been taken over by other Judeans, from lower social classes, who had never gone into exile. Judah turned out to be not the well-to-do home they remembered but a small, struggling backwater when seen in the light of the Babylon experience. Resources were scarce and arguments sprang up.

Such disappointments and dashed expectations inevitably lead to bouts of soul-searching. What could the returnees expect of their future? In particular, what kind of shape might their continuing relationship with their God take? Judah and Israel and their prophets were not inexperienced at coming to terms with disaster and disappointment. The defeats, first of the Northern Kingdom at the hands of the Assyrians and later of Judah itself by the Babylonians, were the cause of major reassessments of the Judeans' understanding of their identity and of their special relationship with God. The vanquished Judah could have taken these defeats as signs either of God's weakness relative to the gods of these mighty empires, or of the withdrawal of God's special favour. Judah's prophets, however, preached that these military defeats were actually signs of God's strength and fundamental commitment. Babylon had been acting as

God's agent, they said, administering God's punishment for Judah's failure to live faithfully by the Torah (e.g. Isaiah 24; Jeremiah 25, 34; Ezekiel 12). When God decided that Judah had been punished enough, and not before, God caused Babylon to be defeated by the Persians and the Persian king, Cyrus, to return God's chosen people to their home (e.g. Isaiah 45). This theological reading of their situation had served the Judeans well in exile. Now they had returned to their ordinary lives, however, the cracks were beginning to show. If Judah had been unable to maintain a faithful life under the Torah prior to the exile, when they were governed by their own king and worshipped at the Temple, who was to say they were likely to do any better now? Would the returnees have to live subject to the constant fear that God might at any time decide that more punishment was needed and subject them to harsh military defeat and another forced removal?

There was another niggling problem. Prior to Judah's defeat at the hands of Babylon, God had made a number of promises. In particular, God had promised David that there would always be one of his sons sitting on the Davidic throne. As time went on after Judah's return from Babylon and the expected reinstatement of the Davidic monarchy failed to materialize, the reality that there would never again be a Davidic king began to sink in. Not only were the people left to face life without this central symbol of their identity as a sovereign nation, they had to concede that God had failed to keep his promise to David. If God had failed to keep that promise, who was to say that any of God's promises would prove to be reliable?

As we've seen, Genesis 15 was probably written, or at least substantially edited, during this post-exilic period. Probably this rather odd chapter, in which not much action happens, was written to address just these problems being faced by the Judean returnees. Let's see what solutions the chapter proposes.

'Do not be afraid, Abram . . .'

At the opening of Genesis 15 God comes to Abraham in a vision and makes a speech designed to comfort and reassure him. Abraham responds not with thanks but by voicing his worries about his lack of a son. Over two verses Abraham makes it clear that he is not impressed with promise of reward when he lacks a son to whom to pass it on. God responds in return by telling Abraham that he will have a son to be his heir; what's more, Abraham will have a multitude of descendants, so many that they will be as impossible to number as the stars of the sky. God demonstrates this promise by taking Abraham outdoors to look at the stars and to marvel at their number. This is the point at which the text gives us the celebrated statement of Abraham's belief, and the reckoning of it to him as righteousness.

But the story is not over here. God's promises to Abraham include not only descendants but also land. In the very next verse God repeats the land promise, telling Abraham that he is the one who brought Abraham out from Ur of the Chaldeans, and that he did so in order to give him 'this land' to possess. Does Abraham respond with belief and gratitude? No, he does not. In fact, the response of this 'giant of faith' sounds almost wheedling, 'O Lord GOD, how am I to know that I shall possess it?' God responds with another practical demonstration, this time a very odd one indeed. God instructs Abraham to bring three sacrificial animals and two birds. Abraham immediately does so and cuts the animals in half, laying the two halves side by side. He does not cut the birds. When birds of prey come down to feast on the carcasses, Abraham drives them away. Later 'a smoking fire-pot and a flaming torch' pass between the pieces of the animals that Abraham separated and God repeats the land promise, but this time using the language of covenant.

For twenty-first-century readers this story is very strange. What are we to make of this antiquated and frankly unsavoury ritual? And what are we to make of the complaining, uncertain Abraham?

One way of finding some answers to these questions is to ask ourselves what the earliest readers (or hearers, for these stories were often read aloud) would have made of this text. What necessary context, unavailable to us, would have helped them to make sense of this story? There is a great deal going on under the surface of Genesis 15 that is mostly unintelligible to us but that would have conveyed important information and messages to its first audiences.

'Which Bank?'

Some years ago in Australia the Commonwealth Bank ran a series of advertisements in which they established a tag line – 'Which Bank?' Each advert introduced a scenario in which a bank came through for its customers, followed by the question 'Which Bank?' and a picture of the Commonwealth Bank's logo. The adverts were extremely successful, so that nearly all Australians came to associate the words 'Which Bank?' with the Commonwealth Bank. Eventually, the later adverts only needed to contain the words 'Which Bank?' to be effective. Even today, all an Australian needs to hear is 'Which Bank?' to recognize an allusion to the particular bank and its advertising strategy. For a non-Australian, however, the words 'Which Bank?' are likely to be meaningless. Familiarity with the necessary background context can be vital for making sense of text.

It is the same with Genesis 15. Let's start with the strange ritual of the birds and animals. The only mention of a similar ritual in the Old Testament is found in Jeremiah 34, where it is connected with Jeremiah's prophecy of the Babylonian exile. King Zedekiah had made a covenant with all the people of

Jerusalem. Under the covenant, the people should all set free their Hebrew slaves. At first the people kept the covenant and set their slaves free, but almost immediately they enslaved them again. God told Jeremiah that just as the people had not kept this covenant, he would not keep his covenant with Judah.

> And those who transgressed my covenant and did not keep the terms of the covenant that they made before me, I will make like the calf when they cut it in two and passed between its parts: the officials of Judah, the officials of Jerusalem, the eunuchs, the priests, and all the people of the land who passed between the parts of the calf shall be handed over to their enemies and to those who seek their lives. Their corpses shall become food for the birds of the air and the wild animals of the earth.   (Jer. 34.18–20)

Here, the action of passing through the parts of the calf is part of a curse that befalls the covenant partners who break the covenant. They will be given to their enemies and their corpses will be eaten by birds and animals. How does this relate to the ritual in Genesis 15? The key is that the smoking fire-pot and flaming torch that pass between the pieces in Genesis 15.17 are symbols of God. The fire and smoke represent the ways in which God manifested himself in the rescue of the Israelites from Egypt and at the covenant ceremony at Mount Sinai. In Genesis 15, then, it is God who is depicted as passing through the parts of the animals, and God who takes upon himself the curse of non-fulfilment of the covenant. In other words, God says that he will bear the full responsibility for any failure of the covenant promises and assume all the risk. This is the strongest assurance that God could give that the promises would be reliable.

There is an important difference between this covenant that God makes with Abraham and the covenant made at Sinai. The Sinai covenant was *bilateral*. This means that both parties made promises under the covenant and were responsible for keeping them. God promised to be the Israelites' God, and the Israelites promised to keep God's laws. (See, for example, Exodus 19.3–8.) When Israel failed to keep her side of the bargain, God declared the covenant broken and sent the people into exile. As we've seen, after the return from exile the people became concerned that this might prove to be a recurring pattern. The covenant with Abraham in Genesis 15 is different. It is a *unilateral* covenant. Here the promises and responsibilities are all on God's side. The Israelites can't break this covenant, because there is nothing that it requires them to do! God has effectively swapped places with Israel and assumed all the risk.

You may have noticed that in Jeremiah 34.20 the corpses of those who break the covenant are eaten by wild birds and animals. This doesn't happen in Genesis 15.11. Instead, Abraham drives away the wild birds. Again, there is a hidden allusion. The verb in Genesis 15.11 is *nashab*, which means 'to blow'. Elsewhere in the Old Testament this verb is only used in connection with God – God blows (*nashab*) his 'wind' or 'breath' (the single Hebrew word that expresses both of these is *ruach*). Here it is Abraham who blows, so that the roles are completely reversed – God takes on the role of vulnerable covenant partner while Abraham assumes the role of protector.

The point of all of this complicated allusion is that God takes every step possible to reassure Abraham that God is trustworthy and that the promises are reliable. All of this is by way of response to Abraham's question, 'How can I know?' This, of course, was also Judah's question following the return from exile: 'How can we know that it will be different this time?' And it is often our question too: 'How can I know ... that you are with me, God/that I can do this/that I'm not on the wrong track/that I am safe, etc.?'

There is another allusion to be found in Genesis 15. You might remember that I mentioned Judah's disillusionment in light of the failure of the Davidic monarchy, and God's broken promise that there would always be a descendant of David on David's throne. Something not obvious to a twenty-first-century reader of Genesis 15 is that the chapter is full of royal language that alludes to David and the Davidic promise. When Abraham complains at the beginning of the chapter that he doesn't have a son to be his heir, for example, he is literally saying that he doesn't have a son to establish his dynasty. In Hebrew, Abraham says in verse 2 that he 'walks' childless. 'Walking' before God is what is required of kings (e.g. 1 Kings 2.4; 8.25; 9.4). God's reply in Genesis 15.4 also uses royal language. The Hebrew phrase that is translated into English by the NRSV as 'your very own issue' appears very rarely in the Hebrew text, but it is also used in 2 Samuel 7, the passage mostly widely associated with the Davidic covenant. There God promises David that when he dies God will raise up offspring after him, who will come forth from David's body (i.e. your very own issue) and to whom the kingdom will be given. The editor of Genesis 15 uses these phrases to give the Abraham story additional resonances and perhaps even to introduce theological innovation. For example, Old Testament scholars have suggested that one effect of Genesis 15 seems to be to transfer the Davidic promise of 2 Samuel 7 to the offspring of Abraham. Further, they suggest that this transfer effects a kind of democratizing of the promise in which all Israelites come to share between them the sovereignty that used to attach itself to the monarch.

Even the famous statement about Abraham's belief in Genesis 15.6 contains an allusion to David and the Davidic promise. When the narrator says that Abraham 'believed' God he uses the Hebrew word *'man*. This word can mean both 'to be sure' or 'to believe or trust'. The same word, *'man*, is used in 2 Samuel 7.16, in which God promises that David's house and kingdom will be made 'sure' (*'man*) for ever. By alluding to the failure of God's promise to David, the narrator implies that God's promise to Abraham will not fail.

You can see that Genesis 15 doesn't shy away from the accusation of fifth-century Judeans that God broke the promise made to David. Instead, it confronts the problem directly, if a little obscurely, at least for a twenty-first-century audience. By using royal language and incorporating phrases and images from earlier biblical texts, Genesis 15 acknowledges the failure of the Davidic promise at the same time as it revitalizes and renews the promise by addressing it to Abraham.

The promise

As I've already suggested, Genesis 15 is not so much about Abraham's extraordinary belief or trust as it is about the measures taken by God to assure Abraham that belief or trust is the right response. The focus of the chapter is not Abraham's faith but God's faithfulness. Ironically, it is Abraham's uncertainty, or even doubt, that makes this possible. His doubts and questions allow God the opportunity to show the lengths to which he will go to assure his chosen servant that he, God, is trustworthy and that his promises are reliable.

This was an important message for the earliest audience of Genesis 15. This story would have reassured post-exilic Judeans that God was still in charge. The promises were still valid, but they were being expressed in a new way. Israel would no longer bear all the vulnerability in her relationship with God. Instead, God was taking all the risk of the relationship upon himself. It wasn't inevitable that Judah would experience further military defeats or forced exiles because the future of Judah's relationship with God was no longer dependent upon Judah's keeping of the law. What's more, Judah should reconceive her hope for a renewal of the monarchy and understand that Judah's sovereignty had not been lost. Rather, it would continue to be expressed through the whole people of Judah.

And for us? What can Genesis 15 mean for us – especially in these early days of our journey through Lent? Genesis 15 is reassuring for us also, I suggest, especially if it means that we don't need to hold Abraham up as a towering model of faith. The driving force of the story is not Abraham's belief but, rather surprisingly, his fears and vulnerabilities. Our fears and vulnerabilities are also driving forces in our lives. If we are able to understand that Abraham is like us in this regard, and that God remained faithful to him *not because of his great faith, but despite his rather ordinary limitations*, then Genesis becomes for us a wonderful story of God's faithfulness and reliability. What is extraordinary here is not Abraham's great faith, but the lengths God goes to in order to make his love known to his chosen one.

Instead of worrying that our commitment to our Lenten discipline is not strong enough, or that our faith is not sure enough, this story reminds us that our relationship with God is not wholly dependent on us. Instead, God is working all the time to find ways to be in relationship with us. In fact, it can often be when we feel that our faith is at its lowest ebb that we are in a position to recognize this. Earlier I mentioned the years that I spent living with ME and my frustrations at being unable to respond fully to what I believed to be God's call to me. I wish I could say that I was a paragon of faithfulness during all those years, but in truth I wasn't much of a paragon of anything. I tried a whole series of potential 'cures', some of which were every bit as strange as the ritual of the birds and animals in Genesis 15! Some things, like meditation, were very helpful. Others just cost a lot of money and made me feel a bit silly. Over time I began to believe that I would simply have to resign myself to being unwell for good. I decided that God was either unable or unwilling to help.

I was wrong. Help arrived suddenly and dramatically and just when I needed it. I was offered a dream job working for an archbishop. The only problem was that it was a full-time job and meant moving to a new city. I'd spent the last decade adjusting to working only a few hours every week – I was crazy even to consider it! *But,* three days previously I had read about an opportunity to participate in a new intensive exercise programme designed to help people with ME. I figured that if I had the job I'd be able to afford the (very) expensive exercise programme. *And* if I'd done the exercise programme perhaps I could take the huge risk of accepting the job. I prayed and made lots of inquiries. The dates all seemed to work out, so I talked to the Archbishop and somehow convinced him that I was worth the risk. I took the job and it was everything I hoped it would be. I can't say that it was really easy. For the first year or two I did nothing but work and rest. But I managed, and gradually I recovered. Even now I'm not entirely free of ME. It pops up when I'm especially tired or stressed so I have to take care of myself. But I no longer think of myself as a sick person, and I now have all the energy I need to take on the tasks that I think God might be calling me to.

I lost faith in God, but God hadn't lost faith in me. Genesis 15 reminds me of that experience and assures me that mine is not an isolated case. God is faithful to all his people, no matter if they lose sight of that for a while. The vulnerable, unsure Abraham is a much more helpful model for me than the 'champion of faith' Abraham, because he shows me who God is.

For all these reasons, Genesis 15 is a pretty good story to have up your sleeve when you hit week two. The crucial elements of the story are God's promises to Abraham and his response of love to Abraham's fears and vulnerabilities. No matter our fears and our concerns and our sense that we are somehow missing some element that is crucial if we are to travel the journey – God still promises to be on the journey with us. This promise is not dependent on our being especially brave or capable or faithful. We do not have to possess any particular quality in order to attract God's favour. Like Abraham in Ur of the Chaldeans, God chooses us simply because we are his creatures, and not because of our attributes. This is something we all need to remember, because there are times when God just seems to be absent. Sometimes, however, quite unexpectedly, God shows up. Next week's story is about one of those times.

Questions for reflection

For individuals

1 What Lenten discipline have you set yourself? How is it going? Have you been experiencing 'week two' syndrome? If so, has it led you to lose faith in God?
2 Can you remember a time when you thought that God had forgotten you, and when neither your own efforts nor prayer seemed to help? What happened?
3 Which Abraham is more a helpful journey companion for you – the Abraham who is a champion of faith, or the one who is a mixed bag of strength, doubt and vulnerability?

For groups

1 Have you set up any rules for your group – such as rules about confidentiality (not speaking of the details of group conversations with outsiders, for example)? What would the group do if a group member broke these rules? Would that member be asked to leave the group or experience some other punishment? If not, how is the integrity of the group to be maintained, and its rules upheld?
2 How does Question 1 relate to Genesis 15 and the covenant agreement between God and Abraham?

3

The visitors
Genesis 18.1–15

How does God 'show up' in your life? People seem to have all sorts of different experiences of God. Some fortunate people have a sense of God's presence being with them all the time. Others say that they are almost never aware of God or of his being present with them. Remarkably, Mother Teresa admitted to being a member of this group. Probably most of us fall somewhere within this spectrum, perhaps being aware of God as both a presence and an absence at different times, or even at the same time. I'm afraid that I usually find myself somewhere near the 'never aware' end of the spectrum, and I constantly need to remind myself, or be reminded, to think about 'where God is for me' in a given situation. This makes the couple of times in my life when God really did emphatically 'show up' all the more remarkable. I'll tell you about one of those times in a moment.

Our story for week three of Lent is one in which God 'shows up' for Abraham. Actually, it is a feature of the Abraham stories that he meets and speaks with God relatively often. When Abraham meets with God they often speak easily, and relatively intimately, as friends. With Abraham there is little of the sense of being in danger that God's presence seems to present to others. Remember, for example, Jacob's surprise at Peniel that his life had been preserved even though he had seen God 'face to face' (Genesis 32.30). Even so, there is something unusually vivid or physically immediate about Abraham's encounter with God here in Genesis 18.

I wonder whether you enjoy Shakespeare's comedies. This week's story shares a feature with them. Shakespeare would sometimes have his characters dress up so that others would not know their real identity. This allowed noblemen and women to pass themselves off as commoners, for example, and family members as strangers. The audience knew a character's true identity, but other characters in the play did not and this opened up all sorts of dramatic and comic possibilities as the audience watched some of the characters labouring under misapprehensions and others obtaining advantages by means of their deception. At the end of the play the deception would be made known and the characters reunited. Something very similar happens here in this week's passage, in which Abraham is visited by God and two of his angels.

In the first verse the narrator tells the reader that 'the LORD appeared to Abraham by the oaks of Mamre as he sat at the entrance of his tent in the heat of the day'. However, when Abraham hears approaching footsteps he looks up and sees three men. The reader knows that it is God who has come to visit, but Abraham can see only men. These different levels of understanding, what Abraham knows and what the reader knows, are maintained throughout the story, so that even for us as readers it can become a little confusing. Sometimes the narrator talks about the visitors as 'them', and sometimes it seems that there is only one visitor, who the narrator calls 'he' or 'the LORD'. Unlike some other stories, God never announces himself to Abraham here. Abraham is left to discover the identity of his visitors (we'll use the plural, for simplicity) himself. This is important, because it means that at least at the beginning Abraham does not know who the visitors are – he only knows that strangers have arrived at his door.

Abraham runs out from his place at the opening of the tent to meet his visitors and he bows towards the ground. He greets the visitors with the title 'my lord', which is formal and respectful but doesn't indicate that he knows they are 'the LORD'. He presses them to stay near his home, where he can offer them refreshment, foot-washing and rest, before they depart again in the cool of the afternoon. The visitors agree and Abraham rushes off to prepare a meal for them.

Even in this story, where God's appearance to Abraham is 'fleshed out', so to speak, there is an element of mystery about both the nature of the visitors and Abraham's perception of them. It is rather like our lives, in which we often have difficulty discerning whether it is God who is acting or just other people. In this story even Abraham is unable to discern clearly. The mystery does get cleared up by the end of the story, so that by the time Abraham is standing opposite God and bargaining with him to save the people of Sodom (Genesis 18.22–33), both the reader and Abraham know that it is God that Abraham is talking with. We know this because Abraham uses an address that approximates to 'the LORD' in Genesis 18.27, 30, 31 and 32, and refers to God as 'the Judge of all the earth' in Genesis 18.25. But when, exactly, does the penny drop for Abraham? Oh, scholars have argued about this problem for centuries! There really is no clear answer. A few scholars argue that Abraham recognizes God from the very beginning, but most take the view that he realizes only somewhere along the way – they just can't agree about where! It is almost certainly the case that the ambiguity is *meant* to be part of the story. One of the things this story shows us is that the line between meeting God and meeting others can be rather fine.

Christians have often understood the ambiguity about the *number* of Abraham's visitors (one or three?) and their *nature* (divine or human?) as indicating that Abraham's visitors were actually the persons of the Holy Trinity. The idea certainly fits neatly with the contours of the story. This tradition has been especially fruitful for Christian iconography. You may have seen icons that depict the three persons of the Trinity at a meal, with Abraham, their host, peering out from the door of his tent. Almost certainly you will at some time have seen the icon by Russian painter Andrei Rublev, which shows the three persons of the Trinity seated around a table with a space at the front so that the viewer is invited to join them at the table. This image is often connected with the story of Abraham's hospitality in Genesis 18.

Although the idea that Abraham's visitors are the members of the Trinity has been strong in Christian tradition, it is not the only way to understand the story. It is highly unlikely that the Israelite narrator of the story understood it in this way – the Trinity was simply not part of the religious understanding at the time when Genesis 18 was written. On the other hand, stories about offering hospitality to gods or semi-gods were prevalent in the cultures of the nations surrounding ancient Israel. We honour the text when we read it on its own terms and try to free our perceptions of what we know came later. Further, I think that you run the risk of missing some of what the story has to offer if you are too determined to understand the visitors to be the Holy Trinity. For example, you miss the different levels operating in the story, in which you as the reader know one thing and Abraham sees another.

Offering hospitality

Whatever Abraham understands about the nature and number of the visitors, he does what is required of him under these circumstances and offers them hospitality. Now, it is important to bear in mind that in doing so Abraham was playing his role in a well-established set of social conventions. Hospitality was a crucial element of the culture of Abraham's day. Travel tended to happen by foot, and travellers required places where they could obtain shelter and food during long journeys. There were no supermarkets where travellers could stock up, or motels where they could find safe lodging for the night, so people bore an obligation to make provision for travellers who passed through their area or town. Hospitality performed a dual function. It not only provided food and shelter for vulnerable and hungry travellers, it also protected the areas through which they passed. Hospitality was designed to keep travellers well fed and housed as a way of ensuring that they wouldn't pose a danger, as they might if they were hungry and cold at night. Offering hospitality to a passing traveller was a way of converting a potentially dangerous stranger into an ally.

The traveller was also bound by custom. Once an offer of hospitality had been accepted the guest was required to become entirely subordinate to the host. While the host would be expected to offer the most generous hospitality he could afford, the guest was required to graciously accept whatever was offered, without asking for more, or even showing undue interest in any item in the host's home lest the host feel obligated to make a gift of it! The guest also had one more obligation relevant to Genesis 18 – he was expected to offer some kind of gift in return for the hospitality he'd received. This might be a fairly small gift – a story, some news of events in far-away places or a promise of some kind would do.

Abraham plays his part. Having persuaded the visitors to stay for water, food, rest and foot-washing (typical components of such hospitality) he pulls all the stops out, rushing to ask Sarah to bake flour cakes, having a servant kill a calf, and himself preparing curds and milk. Scholars love to argue about apparently minor details, and they have had a great debate about the quality of Abraham's hospitality! Although some have argued that Abraham could have done more, most have been agreed that Abraham's hospitality was lavish. The slaughter of an animal, for example, was extremely generous and Abraham appears to have been the ideal host.

One of the times when God unexpectedly 'showed up' for me began with an offer of hospitality. I was teaching theology in the College in Melbourne that I mentioned in Chapter 1. We often had visiting scholars from around the world passing through on their study and sabbatical leaves. My boss, the Dean of the Theological School, seemed determined that I should play a special role in offering hospitality to one of them in particular, a New Testament scholar visiting from London. She variously asked me if I'd 'hang around' on the morning he arrived to make sure he was OK, walk him home from a paper he was giving one evening and join her on another evening in taking him out for a restaurant meal. On the evening of the proposed restaurant outing my boss rang my mobile phone an hour before we were due to leave to say that her dog had scratched her eye and she couldn't possibly go out. Would I be prepared to take R. to dinner on my own?

I took him to dinner. We had a terrific evening, talking for hours about all sorts of things that mattered to both of us and that related, mostly, to our work. At the end of the evening I experienced a strong sense that something had happened. I wasn't necessarily sure at that point that the 'something' was *about* R. – it was just that something significant had occurred. During the rest of R.'s stay at the School we had a chance to get to know each other a little better. On one (for me) extremely memorable evening (after I'd duly walked him home from the paper!) we had a conversation about the vocational and life questions that he'd brought with him on his study leave. I found myself suddenly feeling certain that I was going to figure very largely in his answers. It was a feeling that I'd had only once before in my life (it had been connected with the new job that I wrote about in the previous chapter). It was a heavy, portentous feeling of certainty. Now, whether your thing is star signs or Myers-Briggs or the Enneagram, I will always fall into the category of person who is chronically indecisive; as a result, certainty in any of its forms is entirely unfamiliar to me! I knew that it was important not to get too carried away, and that I might be mistaken, but the sense of certainty was strong. Despite the fact that R. had clearly not been visited by any similar sense of portent and had continued to chat away happily while I sat and tried to work out what was happening (!), it turned out that my sense of certainty had been pretty accurate. Eighteen months later I was flying out of Melbourne's Tullamarine Airport on my way to Washington to meet R., and then on to London to marry him . . .

Now, you might be tempted to object that this isn't a story about God but merely one about falling in love or even simple wishful thinking. No doubt both those things were involved – I suggested in Chapter 1 that God and our own desires often get mixed up together – but it was something else as well. As I say, I'd experienced this feeling once before and there the context had been closely connected with vocation. It was the same this time. Meeting and marrying R. has meant leaving behind my work as well as my family and friends, and a new life in London has seen significant changes and developments in how I live out my sense of call.

One of the reasons why this event made such an impact upon me was that, like many single women today, I had spent many years (decades, even) longing to find a partner. I had a rich and fulfilling life, but I wanted to be able to share it and to experience the day-to-day routine of life with another person. I had single friends with the same longing, and others who longed for different things. I wonder whether there is a longing in your life: for a partner, to find a job, to trace birth parents, to find a lost child, to return to the country of your birth, for example. These gaps in our lives, and the longing to fill them, can be extraordinarily powerful, and most of us have at least one, even if we keep it well hidden.

One of the strongest forms of longing that I have encountered in some of my friends is the desire to have a child. Having children is something that is programmed into us. The desire has to be strong so that we are motivated to take on the gargantuan task of raising another person. This can make it excruciatingly painful if we, like Sarah and Abraham, find ourselves unable to have a child. The desire also reminds us that we are human beings, who are clever and powerful in many ways but who are still subject to the laws of nature. Although we have taken great strides in the provision of fertility treatments, childlessness is not a problem that can be solved merely by spending money on it.

Meanwhile, back in Mamre . . .

It is significant that the pathway to unexpected change, for me, was the offering of hospitality (even if it was rather pushed on me by my boss!). Abraham's hospitality also heralded unexpected change. You will remember from Chapter 2's discussion of Genesis 15 that the primary tension driving Abraham's story was his lack of a son to be his heir. Childlessness was Abraham's particular longing, but it had an unusual extra twist because without an heir Abraham did not see how any of God's other promises could be realized. In Genesis 15 God assured Abraham that no one but Abraham's 'very own issue' would be his heir (15.4).

Abraham's need for an heir is still a driving issue here in Genesis 18. We need, however, to backtrack a little over the parts of the story that we have missed. After having lived in Canaan for ten years Sarah still has not conceived a child. The very first thing we learn about Sarah is that she is barren and childless (Genesis 11.30), and the further ten years without a child (in a culture without contraceptives), together with her increasing age, seem to militate against any chance that she might ever conceive in the future. Sarah herself attributes her barrenness to God (Genesis 16.2), so she comes up with a plan to overcome her affliction. She will send her Egyptian maidservant, Hagar, to Abraham in order that Hagar might have Abraham's child on Sarah's behalf. This story is quite 'modern' in the sense that childless women and men still explore essentially similar approaches to having a child. Surrogacy arrangements, like this one, IVF and donation of eggs and sperm are all methods that we use to try to help nature do its job.

When presented with Sarah's plan Abraham listens to his wife and it all goes ahead. Unfortunately, Sarah has not thought through all of the likely consequences of her plan. When Hagar duly conceives she apparently recognizes the tactical advantage that she has achieved over her mistress and she looks upon Sarah with contempt (Genesis 16.5). Sarah again turns to Abraham, who appears to abdicate responsibility for Hagar, pretty much as he had previously abdicated responsibility for Sarah during their sojourn in Egypt (Genesis 12.10–20). Abraham tells Sarah to do as she pleases. Sarah treats Hagar badly and the pregnant Hagar flees (16.6).

Hagar is 'found' by the angel of the Lord by a spring of water in the wilderness. The angel tells her to return to Sarah and submit to her. Just as there is ambiguity about the nature of Abraham's visitors in Genesis 18, so there is ambiguity about the identity of the angel in Genesis 16. By verse 13 it becomes clear that it is actually God to whom Hagar is speaking. God tells Hagar to name her son Ishmael, meaning 'God hears' or 'God will hear'. Then, extraordinarily, *Hagar gives God a name*. She calls God 'El Roi', or 'God who sees'. You can see how closely related these two names are! The act of naming was thought by the Israelites to generate special power, so that the person doing the naming acquired a certain power or influence over the person being named. You will remember that in Genesis 2, for example, the human creature names the animals. For the text to tell us, without any sense of disapproval, that a non-Israelite woman gives God a name is entirely unexpected.

The text doesn't explicitly say that Hagar returns to Sarah and Abraham. It seems that she does so, however, and that she gives birth to Abraham's 'firstborn', Ishmael. Abraham and Sarah have the child they wanted. Everybody (other than Hagar) is now happy.

It is hard to imagine, then, how Abraham feels in Genesis 17 when, thirteen years later, God appears and promises to give him a son by Sarah. Initially, Abraham is so surprised that he falls on his face and laughs! Instead of thanking God, Abraham intercedes on behalf of his other son, Ishmael. Abraham and Sarah have had plenty of time to become attached to Ishmael and to get used to being a one-child family. Because we as readers know that Isaac is the child of promise, and a miracle baby, we tend to imagine that Abraham easily shifts his allegiance to the new child. In fact, Abraham and Sarah face the unexpected problems also faced by current-day parents who, having adopted a much-wanted child or had their own by IVF, donation or surrogacy arrangement, find themselves falling pregnant naturally. There is joy certainly (after the initial shock!) but also concern about how they are to treat both children equally, and to persuade both that they are valued and loved. In Abraham and Sarah's case this concern is magnified by the fact that God is determined to treat the two boys differently. God chooses Isaac, but excludes Ishmael from his covenant with Abraham and his descendants.

The gift

When I was talking about the conventions of hospitality in the Ancient Near East earlier, I said that there was one final thing expected of a guest – he was expected to give his host a gift. This was a way of 'evening up the score' (even if the gift was of no monetary value) so that there was no outstanding sense of obligation that might possibly lead to violence between host and guest. Here in Genesis 18 Abraham's guests give him a gift. The gift is a repeat of the promise that Sarah will have a son. 'I will surely return to you in due season, and your wife Sarah shall have a son' (Genesis 18.10). Now it is Sarah's turn to laugh! We'll come back to Sarah's response in a moment.

What do you think about Sarah and Abraham's situation, with the promise of this new son? Do you, perhaps, question whether Sarah and Abraham were right to pursue the surrogacy option with Hagar? Does the renewed promise of a son suggest that they were wrong to try to find their own solution? Is Abraham's role in all of this perhaps a further instance of the scepticism, or lack of faithfulness, that he displayed in Genesis 15? We need not see it this way, I'd suggest. Sarah and Abraham took matters into their own hands. Despite several years having passed God had not given Abraham and Sarah a son, and so they took the initiative. Remember that their solution matched God's promise in Genesis 15.4: 'no one but your very own issue shall be your heir'. Ishmael was Abraham's 'very own issue', even if he was not Sarah's son.

Cast your mind back to the first week of Lent, when we were thinking about Genesis 12 and the issue of discerning call and vocation. Do you remember that I suggested that when we are becalmed we may need to take some action, to 'set out', and that we may need to do this even if we're unsure about the direction in which we should be travelling? Well, Sarah's plan can be thought of as just such a 'setting out'. It would be an understatement to say that things did not initially go smoothly (especially for Hagar!). But what was the longer-term outcome? The most immediate thing that we might notice is that Ishmael's birth is followed immediately in the text by two stories in which the promise of a son for Abraham is repeated. In each case the promise is intensified in the sense that there is a time-frame given (12 months in each case) and it is made clear that Sarah is to be the child's mother. In that sense, it seems that in 'setting out' Sarah and Abraham caught a breeze that led to the outcome they were hoping for, if not quite in the way they'd anticipated.

What about the long-term impact of Sarah's plan? We shall see, next week, that after having no heir Abraham suddenly finds himself with two! We have heard already that God distinguishes between the two sons in Genesis 17. Isaac will stand within the covenant and inherit the divine promises from Abraham, but Ishmael will not (we'll find out a little more about the implications of this in Chapter 4). In one sense, then, Ishmael is born into a situation of inequality. However, this is not to say that Ishmael is not important to God, or that he will not receive God's blessing. Although Ishmael will not be a member of the covenant people, God does make promises in respect of Ishmael and some of them are the same as the original promises to Abraham! For example, God promises to make Ishmael a 'great nation' (Genesis 17.20, cf. 12.2). In a similar vein, God promises Hagar that he will 'so greatly multiply your offspring that they cannot be counted for multitude' (Genesis 16.10). This promise resonates with God's promise to Abraham in Genesis

15.5. 'Look towards heaven and count the stars, if you are able to count them . . . So shall your descendants be.'

In Chapter 1 I suggested that when we unilaterally 'set out', or when we think that we are taking action in response to a call but realize later that we have misunderstood the nature of the call, we set in play events that God later weaves into a new version of our future. We can see this at play in Abraham's story. In Genesis 17 God amends, or expands, a promise to Abraham. In Genesis 12.2 God had promised to make Abraham a great nation. In Genesis 17.4 God makes a subtle but significant change to this promise, telling Abraham that he will be 'the father of *a multitude of nations*'. (This change is also reflected in the change of name in Genesis 17.5 from 'Abram', meaning 'father of many', to 'Abraham', meaning 'father of many people(s)'.) The birth of Ishmael changes and enriches Abraham's legacy. Abraham becomes the ancestor not merely of a single nation but of many nations. Today, we remember Abraham as the ancestor of all three great monotheistic faiths – Judaism and Christianity through Isaac and Islam through Ishmael – and the first great 'ecumenist' (builder of friendship and relationship across faith boundaries). We will go on to explore some questions about the relationships between Abraham's children in coming chapters. In Chapter 4 we will look at the relationship between his two sons. In Chapter 6 we will look at the relationship between today's descendants of Abraham and ask how we can live together and share God's world.

Ishmael is by no means an interloper or second-class citizen in God's long-term plan. His existence transforms both Abraham's legacy and the world that we know. This is the way in which God acts in our lives with, around and sometimes despite our actions. As I said back in Chapter 1, in God's economy nothing is wasted. So it will be also with you when you 'start out' or point your bow out to sea in order to catch the breeze you need to get you going again. You cannot know what the consequences will be, and they may be disconcerting or even astonishing, but you can know that God will work with them and weave them into your story.

What do you do when God 'shows up'?

Earlier I said that I experienced God 'showing up' in the circumstances of meeting my husband. I jumped over the next part, allowing you to believe that the 18 months between meeting and my leaving for London had all been smooth sailing! In some ways, it did all go remarkably smoothly, given that we were 'dating' from opposite sides of the planet. We survived by spending a lot of time on Skype and meeting at biblical conferences held on continents somewhere between us, whenever possible. In other ways it did not go smoothly at all, especially early on. Some of my friends laughed at me! They were not all impressed with my choice of partner, and a number let me know that they didn't approve or that I only had to say the word and they would ride in and save me from R.'s evil clutches! Even I wasn't really sure how I felt about it all sometimes, which was not helped by all sorts of unexpected reactions arising in me. Initially I didn't sleep for several weeks, I completely lost my appetite (a very new experience for me!) and, most oddly, my fingernails split and broke in a way they've not done before or since. I felt afraid, and my fear expressed itself sometimes as anxiety and sometimes as anger. My behaviour became erratic and I am fortunate that R. was patient with me and was able to sift through the mess of mixed signals that I was sending him.

I take heart from the fact that neither Abraham nor Sarah reacted terrifically well to the visitors' gift of a renewed promise that they would have a son. The two of them, quite independently, reacted with incongruous laughter (Abraham in Genesis 17.17 and

Sarah in 18.12). In each case their laughter reflects an incredulity that they should produce a child at their advanced ages. Abraham falls on his face as he laughs, saying, 'Can a child be born to a man who is a hundred years old? Can Sarah, who is ninety years old, bear a child?' He seems genuinely unable to comprehend that God should still intend to give them a son. His first words are not about the promised son at all, but a request that Ishmael might live in God's sight (Genesis 17.18). Sarah doesn't react quite so physically, but laughs inwardly. 'After I have grown old,' she says, 'and my husband is old, shall I have pleasure?' Despite Sarah's relatively contained reaction, God hears her. He says to Abraham, 'Why did Sarah laugh, and say, "Shall I indeed bear a child, now that I am old?" Is anything too wonderful for the LORD?'

Sarah is afraid – afraid and embarrassed about having been caught out by God. She makes the situation worse by denying that she had laughed. Her denial doesn't work, and the story closes with God's rather chilling final line, 'Oh yes, you did laugh.'

The story tells us that giving a child to a couple who are both old and infertile is not too wonderful for God. The impossible is, apparently, possible with God. It is all, however, altogether too wonderful for Sarah to take in and, like mine, her reaction is fearful. God's imagination is greater than yours or mine. What you or I may perceive as being beyond the realms of the possible is not so for God. (It may take us a while to catch up emotionally, of course!)

How are we to understand this in our own circumstances? How are we, for example, to hear the message that nothing is impossible with God when we have been living with a longing, or an illness, or a grief for many years, or even decades, without having found healing? I don't have a simple answer for you. I do know that my prayer for a partner was answered by God after many decades and long after I had given up the cause as lost. If you are living with a long-unanswered prayer, however, the last thing you will want is to have me tell you not to worry because it all worked out for me! It is quite likely that you also have experience of your own to draw on. Have there been protracted periods of sadness, illness, loss or other hardship in your life that you thought would never lift but which did eventually change? Can you remember how the change came about? Did something happen that was unexpected, or were you at some point able to look back and see that things had changed, perhaps imperceptibly, over time? When the change came, was the outcome what you had hoped for? Or was the outcome something different, but which healed the brokenness in you nevertheless? Did it send you in any unexpected directions?

The extraordinary comes out of the ordinary

I don't have any simple answers for you, but I do have a difficult one. Genesis 18 grounds the extraordinary idea that God can do the impossible in our lives in a healthy foundation of everyday realism. The renewed promise of a son does not come to Abraham and Sarah in the context of something dramatic that they do. On the contrary, it comes as they patiently and faithfully do what is expected of them in terms of the hospitality code that binds them. Most likely the visit by these visitors was not an isolated case, but only one of many to which Abraham and Sarah found themselves called to respond. It is impossible to know what their feelings were about their obligation to provide hospitality to passing strangers. Perhaps Abraham resented feeling bound to offer to these particular strangers a calf that he had been saving for a special occasion for his household. Perhaps Sarah resented being called upon to bake at a moment's notice. The text doesn't say. It merely suggests that when confronted by a group of travelling strangers, Abraham responded with vigour and generosity. Abraham didn't know at the outset that the visitors were God and two of his angels (see Genesis 19.1 where the two men who go on to Sodom are called 'angels'). The New Testament author of Hebrews 13.2 almost certainly had this story in mind when he wrote that we 'should not neglect to show hospitality to strangers, for by doing that some have entertained angels without knowing it'.

Abraham and Sarah would not have expected any immediate reward for playing by the rules of the hospitality code. Guests will have come and gone, and no doubt during some of Abraham's travels through Canaan (for example, in Genesis 12—13) he will have been a stranger himself, receiving hospitality at the hands of others. For sure, they could expect guests to offer a gift to 'repay' them for their kindness. However, such a gift might amount to little more than a snippet of news or a story from afar. Abraham did not bow to the ground, kill a calf and mobilize his household to cook for his visitors because he hoped to receive a reward for his efforts. He did it because it was expected of him and because it was kind – and there is every indication that he did it with warmth and generosity.

In just the same way, we had many academic guests come through the university college where I met my husband-to-be. Over a number of years I had offered hospitality to a large number of them. Often I was richly rewarded in meeting truly impressive women and men. Sometimes there wasn't much obvious reward at all. Nevertheless, offering hospitality was something I did for visitors because it was expected of me and because it was a civilized and kind thing to do. R.'s visit promised no particular gift for me. In fact early indications suggested to me that this was a most unpromising guest! It was not until I'd had a chance to really meet him that my early impressions were proved wrong. The gift I received was entirely unexpected.

What can we take away from the story of Abraham's hospitality, into this third week of Lent? Its message to us is twofold,

I think, and both aspects are of value to us as we approach Lent's halfway point. The dramatic aspect of its message is that we have a God who is not limited by the things that limit us. Nothing is impossible with our God. It is therefore important that we don't try to limit God, but keep ourselves open to what he may choose to accomplish in us. This first aspect is tempered by a second, which is that God works within the everyday order and activities of our lives. Our part of the bargain is to undertake our lives and our work faithfully, extending hospitality, generosity and kindness to others, not because of what we might gain thereby but because loving others is part of loving God. This is so even if we are carrying with us long-term unresolved longings, unanswered prayer or unhealed illness. Nine times out of ten we will not be rewarded, apart from knowing that we are doing God's will. Sometimes, however, just sometimes, we will find that we are entertaining angels without knowing it (Hebrews 13.2).

One final thought before we leave Abraham and Sarah for this week. Did you notice that there are some people missing in Genesis 18? Did there seem to you to be an aspect of the story that is just left hanging? What I notice is that we hear nothing of Hagar and her newborn Ishmael. What happened to them? Did they return? Did Sarah and Abraham find room in their newly blessed state to extend hospitality to these particular 'others' and to treat them with kindness? We'll find out next week.

Questions for reflection

For individuals

1 Is there a long-term longing, or unanswered prayer, in your life? Does it have anything to do with the journey you are currently on?

2 What is the hospitality code by which you live? Why do you live by it?

3 When has God 'turned up' in your life? What parts were ordinary? What parts extraordinary? Did you know that it was God, and how did you respond?

For groups

1 Does it matter at what point in the story Abraham realized that his visitor was God? Why?

2 Why did Sarah laugh? What does the narrator think of her laughter? How can you tell?

3 Influenced by this story, Benedictine monastics welcome all visitors to their monasteries as Christ. How might ordinary Christians incorporate this approach in their everyday life?

4

The 'other'
Genesis 21.1–21

It is at about this point in a Lenten journey that we typically begin to focus our attention more keenly upon our destination – the cross and the events leading to the crucifixion. You might be thinking that reading a Lent book about Abraham is unlikely to give you much opportunity to do this! Hopefully, I'll be able to change your mind. Abraham's story, like the Gospels, ends with a devastating narrative about the sacrifice of a son, in which the miraculous return of the son to life brings blessings for the whole world. Sound familiar? The narrative I'm thinking of, the story of the near-sacrifice of Isaac, is found in Genesis 22, which is our text for next week. What we often forget is that Abraham had not one but two sons, and that he was called on to sacrifice *both* of them. This week's story, found in Genesis 21.1–21, is the story of Abraham's sacrifice of his *other* son, Ishmael.

In Genesis 21 the son of promise, Isaac, is finally born. We have been following Abraham's quest to have a son and to find an heir since the very first week of Lent. In Chapter 1 we saw Abraham answer God's call (Genesis 12.1–3), travelling to Canaan with an aging, barren wife and only a nephew to be his heir. In Chapter 2, we saw that after his separation from Lot (Genesis 13.11), Abraham worried that a slave named Eliezer of Damascus would be his heir. God responded with a promise that no one but the issue of Abraham's own body will be his heir (Genesis 15.4). In Chapter 3 we learned that Sarah and Abraham had taken matters into their own hands; Abraham had taken Hagar, Sarah's Egyptian slave-girl, as a second wife (Genesis 16.3) and Hagar had borne Abraham and Sarah a son, Ishmael. In an unexpected turn of events, however, God repeated his promise that Abraham would have a son (Genesis 17.16; 18.10). This time God made it clear that the son would be Sarah's. So when Isaac finally arrives, as he does in today's story, Abraham has a brand new problem – which of his *two* sons is to be his heir? It is a fabulously ironic problem, but no less difficult for that.

What will Abraham now do? Culturally there was an expectation that the firstborn would inherit, and this cultural expectation would later be reflected in the Torah (Deuteronomy 21.15–17). On the other hand, *this* firstborn is half Egyptian *and* God has already said that he will establish his covenant with the younger son, Isaac, and not with Ishmael (Genesis 17.21). How is Abraham to negotiate this problem? And what of Sarah? How will things play out between Sarah and Hagar? Now that Sarah has her own child the power balance between them has shifted and Sarah holds all the cards. Hagar has suddenly become very vulnerable.

There must be a choice between the two boys. One son will be chosen, while the other will not. Genesis is full of pairings like Isaac and Ishmael. One is chosen and the other is not. It starts right back with the first siblings, Cain and Abel. God has regard for Abel's offering but has no regard for Cain's offering. There seems to be no particular reason. It all seems very unfair and it leads to the first instance of murder in the Bible. Here, in Abraham's story, Isaac is chosen over Ishmael because Isaac's mother is Sarah and Ishmael's mother is an Egyptian slave-woman. When Isaac has his own children he has twin boys, Esau and Jacob. Even as they are born there seems to be competition between them to see who will be first to emerge (Genesis 25.24–26)! This time it is less clear who will be chosen, because both boys are the sons of the same mother. The matter is resolved not on the grounds of maternity, but by trickery. The younger son, Jacob, tricks the elder, Esau, out of his birthright. The question of which of Jacob's sons will be chosen is even more complicated – he has not two but 12 sons! Once again there is competition between them (at one point they even gang together and try to kill the second-youngest, Joseph), and the elder sons are overlooked as Judah becomes the favoured one (Genesis 49.1–12).

Reading Genesis 21 is an opportunity to give some thought to the fate of the 'unchosen', or 'other', son. This point in Lent is a good time to think about those who don't, like Sarah, 'hold all the cards'. So far on this journey we have been quite inwardly focused, concentrating primarily on our own stories. This week Abraham's journey leads us to think about the 'other', and about how our own stories can impact the fortunes of others.

Who is the 'other' in our world? You will have a number of immediate thoughts. I want to think about two categories of 'other' in particular. One category includes the 'other' who lives among 'us', such as members of ethnic or religious minorities. The other category includes the 'other' who comes, or who seeks to come, from outside. Nearly every developed country in the Western world is currently struggling with rising numbers of refugees and asylum seekers. This issue will only grow as climate change continues to take its toll on the poorest nations. Such 'others' tend to invoke fear and mistrust in members of majorities, either because they appear to threaten the well-being of the wealthy majority, or simply because difference is unnerving. This level of fear and mistrust only serves to exacerbate problems of financial inequality and restricted access to education, health services, housing and employment.

In most Western countries today Muslim populations find themselves a particular target of fear and mistrust as they are connected in the minds of non-Muslims with Islamist terrorism and violence. They have become the archetypal 'other', whether found 'in our midst' or seeking to enter from outside. In some other parts of the world, including some African nations, opposition, sometimes violent, between Christians and Muslims is a daily reality, and many Western developed nations fear that increased numbers of Muslims will lead to a danger of 'Islamization'. In this week's story we actually read an account of the very beginning of these fears! Today Ishmael is seen as the 'father' of the Arab nations and Muslims look to Abraham as their father *through* Ishmael. Genesis 21, in a sense, represents the parting of the ways between Judaism and Christianity, on the one hand, and Islam on the other. That makes it, for us, a story with current implications.

Being 'other'

Have you noticed that whenever we use the word 'we', we consign a whole lot of people to the category 'they'? 'We' is both a word that includes and a word that excludes. I think about this sometimes during public prayers. Prayers in church are often phrased like this: *we* pray for *those* who are homeless/lonely/ victims of domestic abuse/living with HIV & AIDS/in poverty, etc. I'm not saying that we shouldn't pray like this – obviously anybody suffering for any of these reasons needs and deserves prayer. I'm just noticing one of the effects of prayers of this kind, which is that *we* become the people who pray, while *they* are cast as the people who suffer. When we pray in this way we are able to exist in a kind of benevolent bubble in which we hold ourselves at arm's length from other people who have been unfortunate enough to experience hardship.

My purpose in raising this is to note just how easy it is to cast ourselves in the 'in group' and others in an 'out group'. This is especially true if we happen to be white and comfortably well off and living in a country where most other people look and sound like us. We may go through life without ever having a real experience of experiencing ourselves as 'other'. Have you had such an experience, and did it have a strong impact on you? When I was a child my father visited central Africa and took a domestic flight on a local airline. Afterwards he spoke of his shock and discomfort at finding himself the only white face in a sea of black faces. It caused him to reassess his attitudes about the black people he encountered in his almost exclusively white community. He had got a taste of how it felt to stand out very visibly for just a few hours, and that helped him to understand something of the experience of those who stand out very visibly every moment of every day, just because they happen to live in a country where they are not part of the ethnic majority.

While I was still at primary school my family moved from one part of Australia to another (yes, I know, moving is a constantly recurring theme in my life!) and I went to a new school. It wasn't an easy move. The other children in my class teased, or bullied, me for a number of reasons. One was that I was rather plump and had short, dark, curly hair and skin that turned brown in the sun. They called me one of the most insulting names they could think of – 'aborigine'. I remember that one day the teacher of my class mused out loud about what it would be like for an aboriginal child to join our school. I privately thought that I had something of an idea. In truth, of course, I had had only the tiniest glimpse of what that experience would have been like. I knew that I belonged to the 'in' group, even if my colouring may have given the impression of being at least half-aboriginal.

More recently I've had another experience of being an outsider. Like Abraham I wanted to be an immigrant, and I had to apply for a visa to live in England. At first I explored the possibility of obtaining a visa on the basis of my forthcoming marriage. It all proved to be rather complicated, as we planned to marry in Australia, and the regulations meant that I would be stuck in Australia possibly for months after the wedding while I collected documents and waited for our marriage to be 'assessed' as genuine and not 'sham'. It was sobering to learn that while, as a white, educated Australian, this would take me some time, had I been black and applying to come from an African or Asian country, for example, the process would have been much longer and more arduous. In the end, I discovered that the UK has new and generous provisions making it possible for those with UK ancestry to live and work in the country and I realized that even if I may not have been half-aboriginal I really am half-English (with bits of Welsh and Scottish thrown in). My mother's father was a 'ten-pound pom' who left his home in Cardiff and travelled by ship, 'bound for South Australia', in 1923. I had to collect a lot of evidence for my visa application, but it went very smoothly. Once again I felt for those making an application from Cameroon or Ghana, for example, and who would likely be expected to jump through many more hoops than I had to.

So I have a recent experience of being one of the 'others' coming from outside. Again, it is not really much of an experience of 'otherness'. I look just like everybody around me, even if my cover is blown each time I open my mouth to speak! It is possible that you have had a much more striking or difficult experience of finding yourself an 'other'. How did that come about and what did the experience feel like? Was it a shock?

Did you find, like my father, that it helped you to understand the experience of other people, whether individuals you know personally or larger groups such as asylum seekers? Alternatively, do you consider yourself permanently an 'outsider', whether because of race, or religion, or sexuality or gender? Perhaps you live in a country other than your own and perhaps among people with different coloured skin from your own. If you do, how does that impact upon your everyday life? What would you most like the 'insiders' to know and understand about your experience?

How does the 'other' function in Genesis 21?

This same problem of division between peoples is present in Genesis. Like me, Ishmael is half-and-half. Although he is Abraham's son, he is also half-Egyptian. Prior to the arrival of Isaac it seems that Sarah and Abraham had learned to live with the idea of their half-Egyptian son, despite the initial tension with Hagar. Indeed, as we'll see, the text suggests that Abraham became attached to Ishmael just as he would to any son. He and Sarah both responded to the idea that they would have another son, by Sarah, with laughter. But God kept his promise, and at the appointed time Sarah gave birth to a boy, whom they duly called Isaac (Genesis 21.3). You might remember that names are significant in Genesis, 'Isaac' is no different. It is built on the Hebrew verb 'to laugh', which recalls the laughter of Isaac's parents. When Isaac is born Sarah says, 'God has brought laughter for me; everyone who hears will laugh with me. Who would ever have said to Abraham that Sarah would nurse children?' (Genesis 21.6–7). Sarah has had a year to get used to the idea that she will have her own child, but she is still surprised by it!

Once there are two children everything becomes complicated again. The old rivalries between Sarah and Hagar re-surface as the issue of which of the two boys will become Abraham's heir begins to bite. Now Ishmael's half-Egyptian parentage becomes significant and his place in the family becomes precarious.

As we saw, this issue of 'choosing' between different characters recurs throughout Genesis. In order for one character to be chosen, another must be 'unchosen'. This can sometimes be difficult for us, with our 'egalitarian' outlooks, to understand. Perhaps it might make most sense to those of us with agricultural backgrounds – a family farm can only go to one child, because it would be simply impractical to divide it, especially over many generations. But if we don't have this background the idea that one child should inherit and the other not seems deeply unfair. What are we to make of this theme in Genesis? You might find some background helpful, before we come to the story itself.

The phenomenon of distinguishing between two characters so that one is 'chosen' while the other is 'not chosen' is one of two themes present in Genesis 21 that are also found in stories all the way through Genesis. The other relates to the phenomenon of the would-be mother who is unable to have children. Have you ever noticed that these two themes are very often found in Genesis stories and wondered why? Both have something to do with conventions of Israelite storytelling. The early Israelites told stories in order to understand and build their own identity. No doubt both of these phenomena – having children and then treating them both equally – were part of the ordinary lives of early Israelites, but they also have a lot to do with issues of identity. There were particular reasons why they became especially strong themes in early Israelite stories.

Let's think about the motif of the barren woman for a moment. Why are the biblical stories full of barren would-be-mothers? (Think of Sarah, Rachel, Hannah, Ruth and Elizabeth, for example.) The answer has a lot to do with monotheism.

The early Israelites lived surrounded by peoples of other religions. Many of these were fertility religions. A feature of these religions was the use of fertility figures and rituals to promote childbirth and crop growth. These religious practices must have been attractive to the Israelites, *especially when they were suffering from infertility.* It must have been tempting to think that the god of a fertility religion would have greater power to promote childbirth than Israel's God. By telling stories about infertile women who became mothers, the Israelites were able to explore these temptations and to assert the power of their God.

If the theme of the barren woman is really all about the Israelites choosing God, then the theme of the chosen son is really all about God choosing Israel. The early Israelites were aware that they were only a small people, and that in terms of their region of the world they were quite a young nation. Why, they asked themselves, should God have chosen them rather than some other, better-established nation? What had they done to deserve God's favour? The answer was that there really was no answer. There was no reason for God to choose Israel – he simply had done. (See Deuteronomy 7.6–8, for example.) We saw in Chapter 1 that the same was true of God's choice of Abraham. Telling stories about God choosing between characters and regularly choosing the smaller or younger character, often for no obvious reason, helped Israel to understand God's choice of *them* and his non-choice of *others*. Central to the Israelites' sense of identity was their conviction that God had chosen them to be his special nation. The Genesis stories are foundation stories that help to explain that choice.

The sacrifice of Ishmael

With that background we are now able to come to Genesis 21 itself. While Isaac is still young, Sarah sees Ishmael 'playing' with Isaac (Genesis 21.9). In the Hebrew text, the word 'playing' is based on the verb 'to laugh', and because this verb is associated so closely with Isaac's name, seeing Ishmael 'playing' seems to give rise to a fear in Sarah that Ishmael will try to usurp Isaac. Sarah's words in Genesis 21.10 convey her determination that Ishmael will not inherit along with Isaac. She demands that Abraham cast out both Hagar and Ishmael.

Abraham's reaction is significant. Genesis 21.11 says that Sarah's demand was 'very distressing to Abraham on account of his son'. This is perhaps the strongest statement of Abraham's emotions that we see anywhere in Genesis. There is no matching account of Abraham's feelings when God tells Abraham, in Genesis 22.2, to sacrifice Isaac. In fact, there is nothing explicit in the text about Abraham's feelings about Isaac at all. Sarah appears to have transferred her affections from Ishmael to Isaac. It is by no means clear that Abraham has done the same.

Before Abraham responds to Sarah, God intervenes, telling Abraham not to be distressed on account of Ishmael and Hagar, but to do whatever Sarah tells him (Genesis 21.12). Although God will make Ishmael 'a nation', it is only through Isaac that offspring will be named for Abraham. Whatever Abraham feels for Ishmael, God sides with Sarah in her support of Isaac at Ishmael's expense. Without any argument, Abraham rises early the following morning, gives some bread and water to Hagar and sends her away, along with Ishmael. The two of them wander in the wilderness of Beersheba, in the south.

It doesn't take long for their meagre provisions to run out and Hagar sits down, at a distance from Ishmael so that she won't have to see him die. She lifts up her voice and weeps. You might remember that Ishmael's name means 'God hears'; God does hear Ishmael's voice, and the angel of God speaks with Hagar. He tells her not to fear, because he will make a 'great nation' of Ishmael (Genesis 21.17–18). As we've already seen, God keeps this promise and Ishmael becomes the father of the Arab peoples.

God opens Hagar's eyes and she sees a well of water. She is able to fill the water skin and give Ishmael a drink. Apart from a few observations about Ishmael's longer-term fate, this is the end of the story. Ishmael grows up and lives in the wilderness, where he becomes an expert archer. God is with him (Genesis 21.20). Hagar gets Ishmael a wife from her native Egypt (Genesis 21.21), and that is the last we ever hear of her.

I wonder how you respond to this story. Do you catch yourself thinking, 'It's only Ishmael. It's OK'? Alternatively, are you appalled at the treatment of Hagar in this story and in Genesis 16? Do you feel for Abraham? He clearly has some emotional investment here. Or do you mostly wonder just what exactly this story tells us about God? How should we feel about a God who repeatedly instructs Abraham to allow his wife to mistreat her slave, and not just any slave but one who has borne her a child?

There is no getting away from the fact that this is a disturbing story. Possibly the most disturbing element is God's support of Sarah's demand that Hagar and Ishmael be sent away. God does not appear here as the supporter of the marginalized and oppressed, as we might expect. I'm afraid that these questions about the character of God are only likely to become more acute next week when we read Genesis 22. Having supported the rejection of one son in Genesis 21, God demands the sacrifice of the other in Genesis 22.

It is important, however, not to lose sight of elements of Genesis 21 that point towards some aspects of God that we might find easier to accept. Having supported Hagar and Ishmael's banishment, God comes and finds them in the wilderness, providing water that saves them from death. Clearly the well-being of Hagar and her son is important to God. Being 'unchosen' does not mean, for God, that Ishmael and his mother are not worthy of God's attention. God speaks to Hagar for a second time (remember their previous conversation in the wilderness after Hagar ran away from Sarah in Genesis 16). This in itself is extraordinary – God never speaks to Sarah, for example. It goes further, however, as God renews the promise that Ishmael would become a 'great nation', previously made about Ishmael in Genesis 17.20. God had previously made this same promise to Abraham himself in Genesis 12.2, but he never makes it to Isaac.

What, then, does being chosen mean? And what does it mean to be 'unchosen'? Israel's own sense of herself having been 'chosen' (often referred to as the 'doctrine of election') is one of the aspects of Judaism that we Christians find most difficult, because of an accompanying sense that we are being excluded from God's special favour. Clearly, in Genesis 21, being 'unchosen' does not mean living outside of God's care and compassion. Nor, conversely, does it appear from Genesis 22 that being chosen is all about receiving special privilege. In Genesis 22 Isaac's life is challenged even more directly than Ishmael's life is challenged in Genesis 21. In a similar vein, no one could seriously argue that Jews have been singled out for a privileged and blessed existence! Some argue that 'chosenness' is not so much about being singled out for privilege as being singled out for a special vocation. We need to be a little careful about understanding 'chosenness' in this way, lest we bring too many Christian ideas to our reading, but there are some indications in the text itself that certain characters are indeed chosen for a particular task or role, which is connected with mediating, or bringing, God's blessing to all peoples. We will explore this idea further in Chapter 6.

These thoughts about Ishmael's story may not entirely 'rescue' it for us. There are still elements of it that are difficult to reconcile, but at least this background may help us to understand the story a little better.

The 'other' in our context

In the story, Hagar and Ishmael are cast as 'other'. When we tell our own stories, who do we cast, whether wittingly or unwittingly, as 'other'? In other words, who is the 'they' in our stories? We can ask ourselves this question either about our own personal stories or about the stories of our families, institutions or nations. Just as the ancient Israelites told stories to understand their relationship with God, and through that relationship build their own identity, so do we (individuals, families, institutions and nations) tell stories to help us to build our identities.

Over the last few decades my home country, Australia, has been engaged in an identity-building exercise. This has manifested itself in public debates about Australian 'values' and about how our history (national story) is told. During that time our treatment of the 'other' has not always been something to be proud of. There have been ramifications of our identity-building both for the 'other' in our midst and the 'other' seeking to enter from outside. In relation to the 'other' in our midst, a major part of the debate has concerned the way in which Australia tells the history of its indigenous peoples – aborigines and Torres Strait Islanders. The debate has led to an increased reluctance on the part of white Australia to accept direct responsibility (or 'blame') for the experiences of indigenous Australians since white settlement. This has tended to impact, in turn, on white Australia's preparedness to take the practical steps necessary for reconciliation. Australia's identity-building exercise has also happened at the expense of outsiders – and particularly of refugees seeking to settle there. A focus on protecting an 'Australian way of life' has made it possible for successive governments (of different political persuasions) to promote attitudes of fear about the challenges to that way of life that might follow from a more relaxed attitude to accepting refugees.

No doubt, you will have stories about your own country and the ways in which it treats people as 'others', perhaps partly as the result of an identity-building exercise of its own. If you live in the UK, for example, you will certainly be aware of the UK's refugee issues and of the extraordinary risks that some people are willing to take in order to travel through Europe and finally across the Channel to reach Dover. Instead of people drowning in boats, which is part of the Australian experience (and increasingly the experience of Continental Europe) you will have equally terrible images of refugees falling, frozen, from aeroplanes and from the undercarriages of lorries. As I suggested earlier, all developed Western nations are currently addressing issues about increasing refugee numbers. These numbers will continue to rise, and many countries will be forced to reconsider their attitudes and the extent to which they will be able to continue to exclude people.

Are you aware, in your own context, of ways in which the telling of your national story excludes certain groups of peoples? Who is it that becomes marginalized in order for the dominant group to tell the story of its own identity? Ironically, one of the clearest instances of this phenomenon internationally is closely related to the biblical text, and even to this week's story. Just as Israel was focused on building and maintaining its identity through the post-exilic period, so twentieth- and twenty-first-century Jews have been engaged in identity-building, especially in the aftermath of the horrendous events of the Holocaust. One of their goals has been to establish an independent Jewish state. That goal has been achieved in the creation of the modern-day State of Israel, but it has arguably been achieved at the expense of Arab Palestinians, who have been repatriated into continually shrinking areas of Palestine and whose access into Israeli-controlled lands has been severely curtailed. It is highly ironic that the kind of high-handed treatment to which the ancestors of the Arab peoples were subject at the hand of Sarah is again today a feature of Jewish–Arab relations.

Being family

One of the real gifts of the Abraham story is that it reminds us that despite our divisions we are in fact members of a single family. Jews, Christians and Muslims all trace their origins back to Abraham, through one or other of his sons. Tensions and divisions may have begun to appear very early in the family story, but we are family nonetheless, and the tensions and division that we experience today are in fact nothing new. Over the centuries we have told many different stories about our family history, from a number of different perspectives. But it is the same family history that we tell.

Families always have tensions of one kind or another. The biblical families are no different. Arguments and disagreements, hurts and jealousies lead to the 'othering' of certain family members from time to time. This week, as we enter the second half of Lent, we have had an opportunity to read part of the family story from the perspective of the 'other', and to think about the 'other' in our own families and countries. We've seen that the building of identity can lead to casting people, sometimes quite unintentionally, in the role of 'other'. Sometimes that might go so far as to lead to 'sacrifice' of the 'other', all in the name of the building up of ourselves.

In this book we are focusing a lot on stories and how they function to build identity. We are following Abraham's journey story as a way of reflecting on our own stories and journeys. It is important that we take time along the way to take notice of the ways in which the building of our own identities can have the capacity to marginalize others. If we are able to read stories, including our own, from the perspective of characters other than ourselves, we are better equipped to tell healthy stories that don't set out to build our own identity on top of, or at the expense of, our sisters and brothers.

The other important thing to take away from this week's story, I think, is some reflection about the character of God. The portrayal of God in Genesis 21 is not easy to understand. It will be important to carry some of the questions about God that have begun to develop this week into our reading of next week's story, Genesis 22. But it is equally important to notice the reassuring elements of the portrayal of God in Genesis 21. Just because Ishmael was not 'chosen' but was sent away by his 'chosen' family, that did not mean that God had abandoned him. Instead, God singled Ishmael out for special blessing and promises, and God kept those promises so that Ishmael's family grew to be large and strong.

Next week's story, the story of God's demand to Abraham that he slaughter Isaac, marks the climax of Abraham's journey. We are fast approaching the climax of our own journey through Lent also. If our Christian story is one in which new life comes through death, then we have already begun this week to enter the 'death' phase and next week will take us through its heart. This week has had quite an outward focus, as we've been considering all the ways in which we draw distinctions between people, treating some as 'us' and others 'them'. Next week will be a time for turning inward again, and for facing some difficult questions about the death that we need to die if we are to arrive at the end of our journey and to have life on Easter morning.

Questions for reflection

For individuals

1 Do you find yourself empathizing with one (or two) of the characters in Genesis 21 in particular? Why?
2 Do you come away from Genesis 21 with difficult questions about God? What are they? Do you have answers?
3 What stories do
   (a) you;
   (b) your family;
   (c) your parish;
   (d) your workplace; or
   (e) your nation;
   tell in order to build identity? Who is cast as the 'other' in these stories?

For groups

1 In what ways are the Abraham stories shaped and impacted by Israel's own experience? Can you give some examples?
2 Are the Abraham stories more about exclusion (some are chosen, some are 'unchosen') or inclusion (we are all one family)?
3 Who are the 'others' in your society, or in your church? What causes the 'othering' and how is it expressed?

5

The choice
Genesis 22.1–19

———◆———

When they came to the place that God had shown him, Abraham
built an altar there and laid the wood in order. He bound his
son Isaac, and laid him on the altar, on top of the wood. Then
Abraham reached out his hand and took the knife to kill his son.

(Gen. 22.9–10)

Now we are really approaching the heart of Lent. Holy Week
is looming and it is time to turn our gaze towards Jerusalem
and to begin our meditation on the sacrifice of the beloved son.
'Wait a moment!' you might want to interject, 'I thought we
were journeying with Abraham, not Jesus!' You would be right,
and yet the focus on Jerusalem and on the death of the son is
common to both stories. This week's text, Genesis 22.1–19, tells
of God's extraordinary command to Abraham to sacrifice his
son Isaac, the 'promised one'. Both Abraham's story and that
of Jesus culminate with the death (or near death) of a son. In
both stories God is intimately involved, the scene is Jerusalem
and what is at stake is the future of all peoples. All of these
factors mean that Genesis 22 is truly a story worthy of our
attention in the closing stages of Lent.

You probably know something of this story already. You
may even have strong feelings about it. It is not unusual to have
emotional reactions to Genesis 22. Adjectives like 'monstrous',

'terrible' and 'inhuman' have been used of it. The idea that God would ask a parent to slaughter his or her own child is for many just too gruesome to contemplate. Not being a parent, I can only imagine how having your own children might sharpen your perceptions of this particular story! Even so, I am an aunt to five nieces and I find the idea of God asking me to harm one of them absolutely horrific. At the same time, Genesis 22 has been one of the stories of antiquity that has made the greatest impact on contemporary culture, and that resonates most strongly in our collective imaginations. The many parallels between Genesis 22 and the Gospel accounts of Jesus' crucifixion and resurrection even suggest that it is also possible that the story of the sacrifice of Isaac may have influenced the earliest Christian believers, including the evangelists, in their under-standing of the confusing and traumatic events surrounding Jesus' death and return to life.

In addition to the parallels that we've already seen, there are also some smaller details common to the two stories. Both, for example, involve a three-day journey. In Genesis 22 father and son, priest and victim, walk a three-day journey from their home to the place that God shows them (Genesis 22.2, 4), while in the Gospel accounts Jesus' resurrection is discovered on the morning of the third day. Both stories are set in Jerusalem. Even though Genesis 22 doesn't explicitly mention Jerusalem, a brief comment in 2 Chronicles 3.1 locates Mount Moriah, the place that God shows Abraham in Genesis 22.3, in Jerusalem. A further chilling detail common to the two stories is that in both Genesis 22 and the Gospel, the 'victim' carries the wood on which he is to be killed; Isaac carries the wood for the fire by which he is to be offered as a sacrifice (Genesis 22.6) and, at least in John's Gospel, Jesus carries the cross on which he is to be crucified (John 19.16–17).

These parallels help us to see that our story, the story of the near-sacrifice of Isaac, has strong resonances with the Gospel accounts of the crucifixion, and therefore help us to enter into Jesus' Passion in a new way and from a new perspective. Abraham's story will have been in the forefront of the minds of the first Christian believers, who were also Jews, as they tried to make sense of Jesus' death and rising, and so it is not entirely surprising that we should find echoes of the older Scripture in the Gospel accounts.

Facing the choice

I've called this chapter 'The choice' because in Genesis 22 Abraham faces an awful, or literally 'awe-ful', choice. Put simply, God tells him to sacrifice his own son, and Abraham must choose how to respond. In any ordinary circumstances this would be bad enough, but remember that this is no ordinary son. Our entire journey with Abraham, to this point, has been about God's fulfilment of his promise to give Abraham and Sarah *this* son. Other candidates for the role of Abraham's heir have been rejected (Lot in Genesis 13, Eliezer of Damascus in Genesis 15 and Ishmael in Genesis 17), Sarah's age and barrenness have been miraculously overcome (Genesis 21.1–2) and Abraham has even banished (reluctantly) another beloved son (Ishmael) in order that Isaac might be Abraham's sole heir (Genesis 21.8–21). And as special as Isaac might be to Abraham, Abraham still has more to lose than just a son. God's other promises to Abraham, relating to posterity and land, all depend upon Isaac for their fulfilment, as we've already seen. If Isaac dies, then Abraham will have no descendants through whom these further promises can be fulfilled. In killing Isaac, Abraham stands to lose not just a miracle son but the necessary link to the fulfilment of God's promises. Seen in this light, God's demand that

Abraham sacrifice Isaac appears not only cruel but perverse. Has God spent ten chapters building Abraham up only to cut him off at the knees? Should Abraham really choose to be faithful to such a God?

Recently, I too faced an awful choice. In Chapter 3 I talked about God 'showing up' in the circumstances of my first meeting R., the man who would become my husband. I also spoke of the longing to find a partner that I had experienced for many years and my growing resignation to the idea that this wasn't going to happen. Seen in that light, meeting R. was a joyful fulfilling of my longing. At the same time it created a rather terrible dilemma. Over the same decades when I had been longing for a husband, I had also struggled with illness, and therefore with building a life and career for myself. In Chapter 2 I described my sense of God's faithfulness to me in helping me to find a way to overcome my ME (chronic fatigue syndrome) so that I would be able to take on exciting new work that was being offered to me. That work became one of the most challenging and stimulating experiences of my life. Through it I found myself at the centre of the Anglican Church in Australia. I came to understand how its processes worked, and I got to know its people – influential lay people, priests and bishops. After some years in the role I returned to Melbourne to take up a teaching role and complete my doctoral studies. In the years that followed I found a new place for myself in the academic sphere of church life in Australia. I got to understand the processes of this new sphere and I met its influential people. Rather wonderfully, I found that my contacts and experience from the earlier work helped attract invitations to take on teaching work in dioceses all around Australia. Through this work I was able to share the fruit of my academic writing and research with a range of ordinary Anglicans who had not necessarily done theological study. All of this was extraordinary for the woman who only six or seven years previously had been almost entirely focused on rest and survival!

When I met R. he was about to enter the final decade of his professional life in England. He had the kind of job that couldn't readily be found in Australia. If I was to consider a life with him it would mean sacrificing Australia and the new life that I had carved out for myself, with all of its inside knowledge and contacts. It would also involve turning my back on a group of faithful women and men who had contributed generously to fund my doctoral study in the hope that they were equipping a new female leader for ministry within the Australian church. Had God really showered me with all these blessings only to ask me, and my supporters, to give them all up? Was God 'cutting me off at the knees', just as he seemed to be doing in placing his 'awe-ful' choice before Abraham?

Is God really faithful? Or does he delight in building his people up only to cut them down? Do these questions resonate with you? I asked in Chapter 3 whether you live with a long-term longing that seems to have been forgotten by God. Perhaps, like Abraham, God seemed to offer you an answer to your longing, only to snatch it away again. Or perhaps he offered you (like me) the answer, but in a package that required you to be prepared to give up everything else good in your life to accept it (like the parable of the 'pearl of great value' in Matthew 13.46).

Abraham's 'awe-ful' choice

These questions are placed before us so directly in Genesis 22 that it is important that we consider the story closely. Before we do that, I should point out that Genesis 22 is another one of those stories in which the action happens on a number of levels. Do you remember Genesis 18, where we read about

Abraham's hospitality to travelling strangers? A crucial element of that story is the fact that Abraham only gradually becomes aware of the identity of his visitors. Even though we, the readers, know at the start that 'the LORD' is among Abraham's visitors, Abraham himself realizes this only somewhere along the way. A similar thing happens here. The narrator tells us, the readers, right at the beginning that God 'tested' Abraham (Genesis 22.1). That means that we know from the start that what is to follow is a test, even if we don't know exactly what that might turn out to mean. Abraham, on the other hand, does *not* know that what is to follow is a test. Therefore, when God tells Abraham to offer Isaac as a burnt offering, Abraham understands that God really intends him to do this, and to go through with it. As readers, we know more than Abraham knows, and the narrator knows more than we do. There is yet another level here, which concerns Isaac. Isaac is the one really in the dark here. All he knows is that he is accompanying his father on a journey to make the sacrifice. He doesn't know that he is to be the sacrificial victim.

After that introduction, let's begin at the beginning of the story. God calls to Abraham, saying, 'Take your son, your only son Isaac, whom you love, and go to the land of Moriah, and offer him there as a burnt offering on one of the mountains that I shall show you' (Genesis 22.2). This brief, bald instruction resonates to some extent with God's first instruction to Abraham in Genesis 12, 'Go from your country and your kindred and your father's house . . .' Even some of the language is the same; both instructions use the same direction, 'Go!' (in Hebrew *lek-leka*), the only two instances of this short phrase in the Old Testament. We are reminded, then, in Genesis 22 of Abraham's choice to obey God at the very beginning of his journey.

What does Abraham do? He chooses not to complain, or intercede, or try to bargain with God. He simply gets up early the next morning, collects everything that he will need in order to cut Isaac's throat and to set him alight, and sets out with him and with two of his young men. He walks for three days. Each step of the dreadful journey represents a choice to carry on and to slaughter his child. Each step brings him closer to the moment when he will raise the knife. He could change his mind at any point, yet he continues to walk for three days, placing one foot in front of the other, repeatedly choosing to obey God's extraordinary demand. When he sees the place in the distance he leaves his young men behind to tend to the donkey (Genesis 22.5) and begins the ascent of the mountain with Isaac. Each step closer to the place of sacrifice represents a choice to continue. At any moment he could choose to stop and turn back and so save his son.

What follows is one of the most starkly moving passages of the Bible. Father and son walk on together and when Isaac asks, innocently, about the absence of an animal for sacrifice, his father answers enigmatically, 'God himself will provide the lamb for a burnt-offering, my son' (Genesis 22.8). Despite the pain that this answer must have cost him, Abraham chooses to walk on.

I experienced something of this series of choices as I prepared to leave Australia. At each point I found myself having to choose afresh: when I resigned from my job, when I told my family and one friend after another, when I packed up my house, leaving nearly everything behind and dispatching a miserably small number of boxes to a shipping company. At any point I knew I could change my mind and take the easy choice to stay, but I kept on going – putting one foot ahead of the other. Of course, I wasn't facing the same kind of horror as Abraham, yet every new step was a step that had to be taken consciously and deliberately.

Abraham walks on, until he and Isaac arrive at the appointed place. Abraham builds an altar, covers it with wood, binds his son Isaac and lays him on top of the wood, ready to cut his throat and set him alight (Genesis 22.9). Even at this point Abraham continues to choose, step by step, to obey. He extends his arm, holding the knife. At the last possible moment the angel of the Lord calls from heaven, saying, 'Do not lay your hand on the boy or do anything to him; for now I know that you fear God, since you have not withheld your son, your only son, from me' (Genesis 22.12). At the very last moment, both Abraham and Isaac are saved. God does not want Isaac's death, it seems, but something else. God wants to know whether Abraham feels for him the kind of mix of love and awe that will lead him to obey God's command, even the most gruesome – and God is prepared to take Abraham to the very brink of horror in order to find out.

The next part of the story reminds us of Ishmael's story last week. You might remember that after Hagar left Ishmael to die of dehydration, God opened her eyes and she saw a well of water (Genesis 21.19). In Isaac's story, Abraham looks up and sees a ram (Genesis 22.13). He sacrifices the ram in the place of Isaac. The similarity is not just a matter of chance – a whole string of similarities between the two stories serve to remind us that God had asked Abraham to sacrifice not only Isaac, but Hagar and Ishmael as well.

The angel calls to Abraham a second time and renews the promises to him (Genesis 22.15–18). Abraham has passed the test, and his preparedness to put God's promises at risk leads God to repeat them. There is a slight difference, however. Whereas previously the promises had been given entirely out of the free will of God, now Abraham has done something to deserve them. In Genesis 22.18 the angel tells Abraham that God will fulfil the promises, 'because you have obeyed my voice'. Abraham may have been chosen by God, in Genesis 12, for no particular reason, but in his passing of God's test, Abraham becomes the person that God chose him to be.

At the end of the story we get one more reminder of Ishmael's story. In Genesis 22.19 we learn that Abraham returns to his young men and they go to Beersheba, where Abraham makes his home. Isaac is entirely missing from this final narrative! It is very odd that even though the story is about Isaac's life being placed in jeopardy, and then saved at the last moment, the end of the story has no dramatic fanfare accompanying a joyful and relieved homecoming. If Isaac is missing from the ending of the story, however, then Ishmael is curiously present. The place that Abraham returns to, Beersheba, is the place to which Abraham had banished Ishmael and Hagar in Genesis 21.14. Abraham does not return home joyfully to Sarah. He doesn't even appear to take any notice of Isaac. Instead, he goes to a place where he can mourn the loss of Ishmael. There is a pervading sense of sadness at the end of the story, instead of the joy or relief that might be expected. There is something of an echo of this sadness also in John's account of the resurrection. While other characters rush and run around (John 20.3), some understanding and believing that Jesus who had died has now been raised (John 20.5–9), Mary, who is first to come to the tomb, doesn't understand. She weeps because she believes that somebody has taken Jesus' body away and she doesn't know where they have taken it (John 20.2, 11). It is only later that Mary recognizes the gardener who cares for her in her distress as Jesus, and then goes and shares the news with the disciples.

Our journeys and our choices

What are we, who have set out on our own 'Abraham journey', to make of this difficult story? What does it tell us about God and what God might want from us? In Chapter 1 I encouraged you to understand that you had set out on a journey. I also encouraged you to explore where it might be that God is calling you to travel. Now in the penultimate week of Lent it is time to do two things: to look back and see where you have already travelled and to consider where it is that God wants you to go from here. Having journeyed with Abraham's story, spent time considering God's faithfulness, remembered those times when God unexpectedly 'showed up', and looked outwards to gaze on the face of the 'other', you are now in a position to contemplate the life and the death to which God is calling you.

I have already said something about the choice that I faced when I met R., and about the deaths that I needed to face if I were to choose marriage. There were other deaths to face also. Leaving Australia would mean leaving behind my family, including a father who was about to celebrate his eightieth birthday, my friends, my job, my home and my country. Leaving all of these things would be like dying small deaths. I came to realize that I would also be leaving behind my identity as a single woman, an identity that I'd struggled with for many years and ultimately learned to inhabit and to value. This also would mean dying a death. All of these deaths I would have to die before I could know new life through marriage. Just to complicate things, I came to realize that there would be deaths to experience whatever choice I made. For example, I felt that if I were to choose not to marry R. I would be facing the death of my hope that I would ever marry. I also had a growing sense that if I chose to remain in Australia nothing would be quite as before. Meeting R. had changed everything, so that my old life in Australia could never quite be as it had been before. I was a bit like Abraham, stuck between a rock and a hard place.

Where do you find yourself as we approach the end of Lent and enter Holy Week? Where is your journey taking you, and what deaths do you see ahead of you? Your journey may have brought you to a place where you need to make a choice. It may be that your choice is difficult but that you can see your way through it, even if there is some death to be faced along the way. It could equally be that the choice you face seems impossible, as Abraham's was, and that you cannot see your way ahead at all.

It may be that you are stuck in the depths of Lent, perhaps facing an impossible choice, or perhaps feeling that there are no choices open to you at all. This might be the case, for example, if you are experiencing serious or chronic illness. Of course, in those circumstances it may be that the death you face is not metaphoric, but quite literal. You may also feel that you are without choices if you are the long-term carer for a loved one who is unlikely to see an improvement in his or her condition, and perhaps a gradual deterioration. You may be 'stuck' in a relationship that seems without hope, or that has you caught in a cycle of abuse. You, or a loved one, may be fighting an addiction. You may simply be carrying the weight of an unfulfilled longing for something that appears to be quite impossible, as we discussed in Chapter 3. Your longing may be for work, for home, for intimacy, for a child, or for a number of other things which you lack and without which life feels unpalatable or pointless.

In any one of these cases, Genesis 22 may cut very close to the bone. The God who is presented there may not be the one you need to support you through your trial. You may see in the story a manipulative and uncaring God, not unlike the God who presently seems to be deaf to your prayers. If that is where you currently find yourself I feel a great deal of empathy with you. That was the place I found myself during some of the bleakest times of my illness. There were times when I thought that I would never leave that place.

I'm afraid that I am unable to 'rescue' this story, or the presentation of God in it, for you. If your current experience is that of Good Friday, Genesis 22 is a story that lets you know that you are not alone, but it is not one that lights a clear path towards Easter Day. I can, however, offer a little reflection on the historical context of the story that may help you to understand a little where it comes from.

As I've mentioned in previous chapters, ancient Israel was a small nation, surrounded by a number of older and more established nations and cultures. Israel often borrowed the stories of her neighbours in order to help her to understand her circumstances and to build her identity. Israel almost never borrowed stories verbatim, however, but changed important details so as to make the story, Israel and Israel's God unique. One of the crucial elements that was central and unique to Israel's storytelling and identity-building was the concept of monotheism – the idea that there is only one God. The nations surrounding Israel recognized many gods. These gods lived and loved and fought among each other (not unlike human beings), and the relationships between them impacted upon the lives of humans in a way that helped the ancients to understand some of the more confusing elements of their world. A flood or an earthquake or a drought, for example, could be understood to be the result of a battle between the gods responsible for rain or crops or mountains. In a religion that recognizes multiple gods it is possible to deal out 'good' and 'evil' between them, so that the influence of evil in the world can be explained by the actions of particular gods, while others can be looked to for goodness. When religion is monotheistic, however, so that there is understood to be only one God, 'good' and 'evil' cannot be 'dealt out' in this way. Everything in the world must be attributable to the one God, who must have power and responsibility for life and for death, for good and for evil, and for blessing and for cursing.

As you can probably imagine, this aspect of monotheism raised a host of difficult questions for Israel. Unable to explain misfortune, suffering and evil as either the by-products of fighting between multiple gods or the whims of evil gods, they needed to struggle with questions about how the one God could be both good and responsible for misfortune, suffering and evil. Today's theologians are still struggling with these questions, which are often referred to under the heading of 'theodicy' or, literally, 'the justice of God'. One of the ways that the ancient Israelites dealt with these questions seems to have been to tell stories that explore the problem of a God who is all goodness in a world where suffering and misfortune befall even the 'best' and most innocent of people. The story of Job seems to be one of these stories. There a character called 'the accuser' is used to account for the suffering that God allows to beset the righteous Job. Genesis 22 goes one step further, exploring the possibility that suffering might even be the direct consequence of God's own will and actions.

As I say, none of this helps to 'rescue' this story, or its depiction of God. Nevertheless, the idea that Genesis 22 was conceived and written by people who, like you and me, were struggling with questions about the place of evil and suffering in the world, and the nature of God, may help to give you something of a framework within which to read it.

Becoming Abraham

As I suggested earlier, signs of new life are not obviously apparent in Genesis 22. Although Isaac is saved and although the angel speaks for a second time, renewing the promises to Abraham (Genesis 22.15–18), there is nothing of the joyful or triumphant conclusion to the story that one might expect. Isaac himself is not mentioned, and we are not told that Abraham returns to Sarah. Instead he goes to Beersheba accompanied only by his young men, and he lives there near to the place to which he had banished Ishmael. Genesis tells of no further conversation between God and Abraham, and the very next event in Abraham's life is the death of his wife, Sarah, in Hebron, to the north-east of Beersheba (Genesis 23). Despite the fact that Isaac's life is saved, the end of Genesis 22 has in it something of the sadness reflected in the Gospel accounts of the period between the death of Jesus and his rising from the tomb.

That is not to suggest, however, that there is nothing positive to take from the story at all. There is at least one, slightly uneasy, positive to take out of it. If you cast your mind back to Genesis 12 once again, and to Chapter 1 of this book, you might remember that we saw that the story of God's choice of Abraham gave no hint of a *reason* for God's choice. There was nothing there to indicate that Abraham was chosen because of any particular merit that he possessed. This idea was developed further in Chapter 2, where we saw that despite the famous line adopted by Paul, 'and he believed the LORD and the LORD reckoned it to him as righteousness' (Genesis 15.6), Abraham does not display, in Genesis 15, a particularly remarkable level of faithfulness, but rather appears fearful and uncertain. A similar lack of solid conviction is suggested in the laughter that is the response of both Abraham and Sarah to God's promise of a son (Genesis 17.17; 18.12). Nevertheless, Abraham's hospitality to three passing strangers, whom he does not recognize immediately as God, is excellent, and when God later treats him as a prophet by sharing his plans to destroy the city of Sodom, Abraham's intercession for the people of that city, mostly unknown to him, is forthright and brave (Genesis 18.17, 22–33). The impression that Abraham might be growing into the person God called him to be develops in Genesis 21, where Abraham follows God's directions despite the distress he feels on account of his son Ishmael. Finally, no matter what we might think of God's test in Genesis 22, the sense of the story is that Abraham's preparedness to make the awful sacrifice demanded by God there is indicative of Abraham's maturing in the faith. Abraham might not have been the man God wanted him to be when God first chose him, but in the process of choosing and responding to the call, Abraham becomes that person. I suggested that this positive is 'uneasy' because your feeling about Abraham's obedience, and about the kind of person God apparently wants Abraham to be, will depend upon whether you consider obedience to this type of command to be meritorious or dangerously deluded. Nevertheless, Genesis 22 suggests that a person can grow and develop, so that even if we consider ourselves, when setting out on the Christian journey, to be entirely undeserving of God's regard, we can have confidence that the journey itself will help us to grow and to become the person whom God chose us to be.

In other respects, the new life that follows upon the metaphorical death experienced by Abraham (and the literal death escaped by Isaac!) in Genesis 22 does not become fully apparent until later in Genesis. It is not really until Genesis 26 that the complete picture of that new life begins to take shape. That is where we will travel in the next, and final, chapter of this book. What form will that new life take, and how will it resemble the newness of life that entered the world with the resurrection of Jesus? These are questions for us in the final chapter.

Questions for reflection

For individuals

1 What are your emotional responses to Genesis 22, both immediate and more considered?
2 Have you been, or are you being, asked by God to make an 'awe-ful' choice? What is it?
3 Which aspects of the depiction of God in Genesis 22 do you find challenging? Why?

For groups

1 Is Genesis 22 capable of being a valuable story for people of faith? Why, or why not?
2 Do you think that the Gospel writers might have had Genesis 22 in mind when they wrote their accounts of the crucifixion? What aspects of Genesis 22 lead you to think this?
3 Did Abraham do 'the right thing'?

6

The legacy
Genesis 26

It is Easter Sunday morning in Brisbane, Australia. I am on the deck of a friend's home and the sun is shining and birds are singing as I contemplate the most colourful plastic bucket of gerbera daisies I have ever seen. Some close friends and R.'s two daughters, who are to be bridesmaids, have gathered to make bouquets for our wedding, which begins in a few hours' time. Meanwhile, in a hotel room high above the Brisbane River, my five nieces, who are to be flower-girls, are making their own bouquets and arguing about how they are going to do their hair. Bottles of sparkling wine are being opened and photographs are being taken. At the church another friend is leading the choir through their last rehearsal and my step-mother is putting the final touches on the fabulously over-catered afternoon tea. Everything is in place: my simple dress has survived the journey, the rings have been sewn into my two-year old godson's pocket in readiness for his ring-bearer role, the banns have been read (not strictly necessary, but the description of me as 'spinster of the Parish of St Mary's, Kangaroo Point' went down very well with my London parish!) and somewhere, I know, there is a groom who is generally panicking and doing his best to tame his rogue cravat.

The Easter Day date had been partly intentional and partly fortuitous. We needed to find a time when English guests could get leave to make the long journey, and when our Australian guests could gather from the far-flung ends of the country that had been my home at various times. That meant April, but somehow a Lent wedding didn't seem quite right and Good Friday and Holy Saturday would have been even worse. Travelling the journey of Holy Week has always been important to me, and so Easter Day itself, with all its associations of new life, could be the only day to celebrate such a joyful occasion.

Looking back, I remember that it was tempting to see this day as the culmination of a long journey. Certainly, it had been several years in the making and planning. Now, of course, I know that these years had merely been the first stage in a far, far longer journey, and that the day itself was merely a stage along that journey. A number of significant points had already been reached – I had made the decision to set out, and I had died the death that was part of leaving Australia. In the nearly five months between moving to the UK and the wedding I had begun to live into the new life that was part of being in London, but the 'living into' still had a way to go. Journeys have this tendency to morph and grow as events intervene and goalposts move.

I wonder where you are in your journey. I assured you in the first chapter that there was a journey for you to travel, and that in fact you had already set out. Since then we have travelled some challenging terrain together. Early on we faced the temptations of weariness and lack of conviction, and saw how God assured Abraham at the beginning of his journey that his promises were reliable and that the rewards of faithfulness would be great (Genesis 15, Chapter 2). We have had the chance to observe Abraham and Sarah's doubts, their attempts to take matters into their own hands, and then their reactions when God unexpectedly 'showed up' (Genesis 18). We used their story as an opportunity to remember our own experiences of meeting

God (Chapter 3). Part of the journey has been to turn our focus outward, to become aware of the experience of the 'other' – the alien and the marginalized – both in our own personal spheres and in the wider world (Chapter 4). At this stage we faced some difficult questions about the role and character of God in the story, as we encountered a God who seemed happy to pick and choose favourites and to side with the powerful (Sarah) against the powerless (Hagar and Ishmael). These questions only became more difficult and more acute once we began to walk with Abraham to Moriah, sharing with him the pain of his choice to be faithful to God, a choice that God's 'awe-ful' test forced Abraham to make again and again at each stage of the preparations for the slaughter of his son (Genesis 22, Chapter 5). Finally, this week, we need to ready ourselves to walk into the new light of Easter. Abraham's sad walk away from Moriah was not the end of the story, and in this chapter we will explore the legacy of Abraham's choice to be faithful, both for his own family and more widely.

Before beginning to focus on this week's story, found in Genesis 26, we need to follow the intervening events – the things that happened *after* Abraham's walk back from Moriah. There are some more deaths to witness before we will be in a position to begin to think about new life. The first to die is Sarah (Genesis 23.2). Abraham mourns and weeps for her, and negotiates with the local people to buy a burial cave for her, in Machpelah, east of Mamre where Abraham and Sarah had pitched their tent in Genesis 18. Having mourned and buried Sarah, Abraham's next job is to get a wife for Isaac. He sends his servant to the home of his brother, Nahor (who had remained in Ur of the Chaldeans when the rest of Abraham's family departed for Haran), and there the servant encounters Rebekah by a well. Rebekah agrees to return with him in order to marry Isaac. Genesis 24.62–67 tells us that Isaac brings Rebekah into his mother Sarah's tent, that he marries her and loves her. In this way, 'Isaac was comforted after his mother's death.' To our ears, this final phrase may sound a little 'off' – a little too incestuous for comfort. What it does, however, is to register and mark the movement from one generation to the next. It is a glimpse of the new life that will begin to develop in Isaac and his family.

Then follow the final years of Abraham's life. Abraham marries again, a woman called Keturah (probably of Arab descent), with whom he has six male children (Genesis 25.1–2). Apparently Abraham also takes concubines, although these are not named (Genesis 25.6). Do you remember Sarah's concern that Ishmael should not inherit along with Isaac? Genesis 25.5 tells us that Abraham gave 'all he had' to Isaac, and did not give inheritances but only 'gifts' to the sons of his concubines, before sending them away from Isaac, as he had sent Ishmael away in Genesis 21.14. In Genesis 25.8 Abraham too dies, reportedly at the age of 175.

The stage is *almost* set for Isaac to succeed his father, but first there are some final references to Ishmael. Isaac and Ishmael come together to bury Abraham, in the burial cave that Abraham had bought for Sarah (Genesis 25.9). God's 'favouritism' does not end with Abraham's death. God blesses Isaac (Genesis 25.11), but in a further ironic twist Isaac settles at Be'er-la'hai-roi, the place where Hagar had spoken to God and named him, and received his promises in Genesis 16.7–14 (see Chapter 3). Finally, Ishmael, too, dies (Genesis 25.17), but not before fathering 12 sons, the 12 princes promised to him by God in Genesis 17.20, who become the fathers of the Arab peoples.

In the final half of Genesis 25, Isaac's story begins properly. However, it soon becomes apparent that the new story will be the old story re-told, as the barren Rebekah, with God's help, gives birth to twin boys, Esau and Jacob, who even in their birth, and then again in their youth, struggle with one another to attain the place of firstborn (Genesis 25.19–26).

'Because Abraham obeyed my voice'

With Abraham's death, we are in a position to begin to explore his legacy. We saw in Chapter 5 that Abraham had grown during his life, both in maturity and in faithfulness to God. Although it appears that God didn't choose Abraham because Abraham was particularly special, over time Abraham seems to have 'become' the special person God chose him to be. As Genesis tells the story, the testing of Abraham at Moriah is the point at which Abraham really demonstrates that he has 'grown into' himself, just as someone might 'grow into' a new suit of clothes or a new pair of shoes. Abraham's choice, made over and over again, to be faithful to God, even when faithfulness makes no sense and when Abraham stands to gain no reward over and above simply his own obedience, has long-term consequences. The consequences apply not just to Abraham and to his immediate descendants, but to the whole world.

Reading Genesis 22 in the context of Lent, Holy Week and Easter helps us to see parallels between Abraham's faithfulness and Jesus' own self-sacrifice. Abraham's preparedness to sacrifice Isaac is not unlike Jesus' preparedness to give his own life. (I suspect some parents might feel that Abraham's sacrifice was even the greater – even though I am not a parent, I think that I would choose to die myself rather than be responsible for the death of one of my nieces, or of the godson into whose pocket I sewed our rings on our wedding day.) There are parallels not only between the extraordinary sacrifices made by Abraham and Jesus, but also between the consequences of that sacrifice in each case. The sacrifices made by Abraham, and by Jesus, changed everything. In order to see how that happened in Abraham's case we need to explore Genesis 26.

Genesis 26 seems rather unpromising at first, as it is a re-telling of a story that has already been told about Abraham in Genesis

12, and again in Genesis 20. There is a famine and so Isaac prepares to travel to Egypt in search of food for his family. God intervenes and tells him not to go to Egypt, so he settles instead in Gerar, in the land of the Philistines (as Abraham also had done in the Genesis 20 version of the story). Like his father, Isaac fears for his life on account of his wife's beauty and so he tells the Philistines that Rebekah is his sister, repeating his father's stratagem (Genesis 26.7, cf. Genesis 12.13; 20.2). This time the king of Gerar, Abimelech, is wise to Isaac and discovers the ruse. He becomes afraid and angry. Meanwhile Isaac plants crops and becomes extremely successful and wealthy. Abimelech sends Isaac away, saying, 'You have become too powerful for us' (Genesis 26.16). Despite Isaac's departure, a running feud develops between Isaac's servants and the Philistines when Isaac's servants find a series of wells of fresh water. Eventually Isaac moves a little further away and the feud stops, so that when another well is found there is no more quarrelling. Isaac announces that God has enlarged the land, so that both groups can live in it side by side: 'Now the LORD has made room for us, and we shall be fruitful in the land' (Genesis 26.22).

This story is 'book-ended' with two sets of promises. Both at the very beginning of the chapter and at this point, God appears to Isaac and makes to him promises very like those he had previously made to Abraham. Genesis 26 is like a transition chapter, where the promises God made to Abraham right at the beginning of Abraham's journey (Genesis 12) and then again at other points in the story (such as Genesis 15, 17 and 22) are passed on to Isaac. The first set of promises to Isaac, in vv. 2–5, is particularly significant. God says:

> Reside in this land as an alien, and <u>I will be with you, and will bless you</u>; for to you and to your descendants I will give all these lands, <u>*and I will fulfil the oath that I swore to your father*</u>

> *Abraham*. *I will make your offspring as numerous as the stars of heaven*, and will give to your offspring all these lands; and **all the nations of the earth shall gain blessing for themselves through your offspring**, because Abraham obeyed my voice and kept my charge, my commandments, my statutes, and my laws.
>
> (Gen. 26.2b–6; see below for an explanation of the emphases)

Here God extends to Isaac and Isaac's offspring the promises that he had previously made to Abraham and Abraham's offspring. God's speech is particularly interesting when we compare it with the speech of the angel of the Lord to Abraham in Genesis 22, just after Abraham had sacrificed the ram in the place of Isaac:

> *By myself I have sworn*, says the LORD. Because you have done this, and have not withheld your son, your only son, I will indeed bless you, and *I will make your offspring as numerous as the stars of heaven* and as the sand that is on the seashore. And your offspring shall possess the gate of their enemies, **and by your offspring shall all the nations of the earth gain blessing for themselves**, because you have obeyed my voice.
>
> (Gen. 22.15–18)

Can you spot the similarities between these two speeches? I've marked them so as to bring out the parallels for you. In both speeches there is a reference to God's oath (in italics and underlined), and there are promises to bless Isaac/Abraham (underlined), to make his descendants 'as numerous as the stars of heaven' (italics), and that all the nations of the earth would gain blessing through his offspring (bold). These parallel features have been enough to persuade scholars that the two speeches are connected and that part of the purpose of God's speech to Isaac in Genesis 26 is to extend God's promises in Genesis 22 to Isaac. This idea of extending promises from the father to the son is familiar from the stories of the monarchy in the Old Testament. There is a similar scene in 1 Kings, for example, in which God's promises to David are extended to Solomon after David's death (1 Kings 2.1–4; 9.4–5).

But the extension of the promises from Abraham to Isaac is not the only new thing that is going on here. Not only the recipient of the promises changes here, *but also the foundation, or guarantee, of the promises* changes. Let me explain what I mean. In the first two chapters of this book, when we looked at Genesis 12 and 15, we saw that God's promises to Abraham were free of conditions. That meant that Abraham didn't have a bargain he had to keep before God would fulfil the promises. The conditions were all on God's side. Do you remember the very strange ritual with the animal and bird carcasses in Genesis 15 (Chapter 2)? A smoking fire-pot (representing God) passed between the pieces of the carcasses in a kind of self-curse that was designed to show Abraham that God was taking all the risk of their relationship upon himself. The lack of conditions attached to the promises was important to the biblical writers in the fifth century because, as we saw in Chapter 2, Israel had proven not to be very good at meeting all of God's conditions. The people's failure to keep all of God's laws had eventually led to their being sent away in exile from the land. In telling the story, in Genesis 15, of Abraham's doubts and God's reassurances, the biblical writers were seeking to assure their earliest readers that God's promises to *them* were reliable. They didn't have to worry that their failure to keep God's laws would result in another military defeat and return to exile.

So in Genesis 15 we saw that God's promises to Abraham had no conditions attached. In Genesis 26 there is a change, but in a surprising way. In Genesis 15 God told Abraham that he could rely on the promises because God was reliable. In other words, God's own reliability was presented as the guarantee for his promises. In God's speech to Isaac in Genesis 26.2–6 God presents a new guarantee for the promises. In the future, God's promises would be reliable for two reasons and not just one. The first reason would be the one we're already familiar with – God's promises would be reliable because God was reliable. The second reason related to Abraham. God's promises to Isaac and to Isaac's descendants would, additionally, be reliable *because* of Abraham. In Genesis 26.5 God tells Isaac that he will keep his promises to Isaac *because* Abraham obeyed God's voice and kept God's charge, commandments, statutes and laws.

There is one final step to understanding the change! What does it mean when Genesis 26.5 says that Abraham obeyed God's voice and kept his laws, etc.? Taken at face value the idea makes no sense, because in Abraham's world there *were* no laws! God didn't give the laws to Moses until later in the story, in the book of Exodus. This is a puzzle that has kept Jewish and Christian scholars arguing for centuries! Something that most agree about, though, is that Genesis 26.5 means especially to refer back to what Abraham did at Moriah. In other words, in Genesis 26.5 God tells Isaac that God will extend the promises to Isaac and his descendants *because* of Abraham's willingness to sacrifice his son on Mount Moriah, and *because* of Abraham's willingness to be obedient to God even when there was no possible benefit for him in doing so.

The point of all this long-winded and rather complicated bit of theological analysis of God's speech to Isaac in Genesis 26 (!) is that Abraham's obedience to God in Genesis 22 changes the relationship between God and Abraham's family. Abraham's faithfulness is taken up into, and becomes a part of, God's faithfulness to his chosen people. As a story for Holy Week and Easter, that is surprisingly on the money, I think!

And they all lived happily ever after . . .

I indicated at the beginning of the chapter that I now see our Easter wedding day as the beginning of a journey as well as the culmination of the journey that led to it. Being in relationship is always a continuing process, whether that is relationship with another human being or with God. Will you be surprised to hear that I have moved house again, even since arriving in London from Australia? Fortunately this was only a move across London, rather than one across a country or from one country to another. And this time my husband moved with me. We are still engaged in transition, and have choices to make, as we negotiate more small deaths and look ahead to new life. The journey together is continuing, as we settle into our home, learning how to be two instead of one and how to fit into one another's families.

In the same way, you will be finding that your Lenten journey, whatever shape that journey has taken on, is turning into another, longer, journey that stretches out a long way beyond Easter Monday. Looking back to the beginning of Lent, are you now able to put your finger on the moment you set out? Where was it that you thought you might be headed? Did you get there? Perhaps you are taking a needed break in Haran? Or seeking sanctuary from famine in Egypt? Perhaps, like me, you are engaged in a walking tour of the promised land, mapping out its contours and sizing up the locals. You might feel that you are currently in exile in Babylon, or you could be returning – joyfully or more tentatively. Of course, you may be not just in exile but experiencing your own Calvary. Perhaps a beloved spouse, or child, has died and you have bought a burial cave and are looking forward to joining him or her there one day.

Wherever you find yourself on the map, where is the next part of your journey taking you? If I was right that at the beginning of Lent you had already set out, then it will also be the case that your journey now has a new horizon. Our journeying with God is never done, and you may have climbed a mountain only to discover that you now see a series of ridges of hills beckoning you in the distance. Contrary to what some may think, we are never in this world fully 'saved' in the sense that we can tick the God box and consider our relationship with Jesus a job well done. Even if you have the sense of having arrived at the destination that you were seeking at the beginning of Lent, there will still be a further leg of the journey that God is calling you to walk. There are different ways of looking at this. The open-ended nature of our journey with God might cause you to feel exhausted. Alternatively you might feel a sense of security that your God is big enough to keep you on the road, pointed towards a destination, for the rest of your life.

And what about God's chosen people? How have the journey, and God's blessing, manifested for modern-day Jews? One would have to acknowledge that winning God's special favour has proven to be something of a mixed blessing for Jews. Theirs has been a long history that has embraced both affluence and poverty, and been accompanied by seemingly endless testing and persecution. Even today, with the establishment of the State of Israel, both Israelis and religious Jews still speak of being singled out for special persecution. Relationships between the members of Abraham's wider family – Jews, Christians and Muslims – are also far from being settled and peaceful. The journey of relationship between the three great religions of the book, Judaism, Christianity and Islam, is one that is certainly not over.

'And all the nations of the earth shall gain blessing for themselves through your offspring'

One of the things that Christians often find challenging about Judaism and about the Old Testament is the idea that God chose the ancient Israelites to be his special people. This idea can be a challenging one for Christians if we believe that there is an implication tied up in it that we, as Christians, are not chosen. It can make us feel excluded, in much the same way that Ishmael was excluded when God chose Isaac. It's not great to feel excluded at the best of times, but feeling excluded by God can be particularly problematic! In this chapter so far, I've been talking about what Abraham achieved for his own descendants through Isaac. What about everybody else? What about Abraham's descendants through Ishmael, and what about you and me?

There is in Genesis 26 an illustration of what it means to be 'chosen' by God that might be helpful for us. I'd like to focus our attention on one of the promises that God extends to Isaac in Genesis 26. God promises Isaac that 'all the nations of the earth shall gain blessing for themselves through your offspring' (Genesis 26.4). The angel made this same promise to Abraham in Genesis 22 (Chapter 5), and if you were to go right back to where we started, to Genesis 12.1–3 (Chapter 1), you would see that there God made Abraham a very similar promise: 'in you all the families of the earth shall be blessed'. Actually this promise turns up two further times in Genesis. One is in Genesis 18, just after the story of Abraham's hospitality to the strangers (Genesis 18.18, Chapter 3), and the other is in Genesis 28, where God further extends to Jacob the promises already made to Abraham (Genesis 28.14).

One of the problems with this promise, which I'll call 'the nations promise', is that it is not very easy to work out what it means! The Hebrew here is quite difficult, and each instance of the promise is slightly different. Even once you have a translation that you're happy with, it is still hard to think what it actually might mean in practice. What might it mean for the nations to 'gain blessings for themselves through Isaac's offspring'?

To find out, we need to work through a little more of the Genesis 26 story. In Genesis 26.26 Philistine King Abimelech pays a visit to Isaac, bringing with him his advisor and the commander of his army. Abimelech tells Isaac that he and his people have 'seen plainly' that God has been with Isaac and that God has blessed Isaac (Genesis 26.28–29) and he proposes that they swear an oath and enter into a covenant together. The agreement that Abimelech wants in the covenant is that Isaac will do them no harm, just as Abimelech has done Isaac no harm, but only good. Why do you suppose that Abimelech wants such an agreement? One possibility is that Abimelech is fearful of Isaac and his growing affluence and strength, so that the covenant he is proposing is essentially a non-aggression pact. A further alternative, one that is supported by the story as a whole, is that Abimelech doesn't just want to protect himself from Isaac's remarkable good fortune but wants a slice of it for himself. He can see that the source of Isaac's good fortune is his relationship with God; 'you are now the blessed of the LORD,' he says. Abimelech seems to want his nation to benefit from Isaac's blessedness. Either way, Isaac agrees. Isaac and Abimelech eat a feast together and in the morning they arise and swear the oath and enter into the covenant together. Abimelech and his companions depart in peace (*shalom*).

You may know the Hebrew word *shalom*. It is often translated as 'peace' but it also conveys a sense of wholeness. The word *shalom* is used twice in this story. This is important, because it underlines the fact that in this story two peoples who start out in conflict manage to discuss and resolve their differences and to find a way to live in proximity to one another in peace. What looks on its face to be rather a dull story is really rather remarkable, because although Genesis is a book that records a history of conflicts, between brothers (Cain and Abel, Isaac and Ishmael, Esau and Jacob), between wives (Sarah and Hagar) and even between God and his people (Adam and Eve, the Noah generation), this is the first time that two groups of people are seen to resolve a conflict in such a way as to lead to *shalom*.

We see here an example of what the nations promise may be all about. Here the nations, as represented by Abimelech's people, the Philistines, recognize the closeness between God and Isaac and want to participate in it. They actually come to Isaac to ask to be in relationship with him. In this way the Israelites, represented in the story by Isaac, become both a model for relationship with God and the gateway for accessing God's blessing. The surrounding nations see Israel as an example of God's blessings and decide that they also want to participate in those blessings. The Israelites become the go-between, or the conduit through which God's blessings reach non-Israelites.

This understanding of the nations promise helps us to understand the idea of 'election' – God's choice of Abraham and his descendants through Isaac as his special people – in a way that doesn't feel exclusionary. We discover through this story that God's election is not primarily about choosing a group of people to be specially privileged, but more about choosing a group of people to take on a special role, one aspect of which is communicating and distributing the blessing of God to others.

If we look back, we can see these ideas reflected in Abraham's story. God gave many gifts to Abraham, including his son Isaac, but God certainly didn't give Abraham an easy ride – Abraham wasn't just 'privileged' in any simple way. God treated Abraham as a prophet, warning him what he was going to do in the case of Sodom (Genesis 18.17), and listening to what Abraham had to say in Sodom's defence (Genesis 18.22–33). God tested Abraham, requiring him to give up not just one but both of his sons (Genesis 21 and 22, Chapters 4 and 5). God wanted to know that Abraham was capable of taking on the role that God planned to give him.

We do need to be a little careful about how we understand all of this. It is, of course, rather self-serving to understand the election of Israel as incorporating an element of vocation to the nations, rather than being purely about Israel's own status. The idea appeals to Christians because it suggests that God's choice of Israel is 'about us' nearly as much as it is 'about Israel' and it helps us not to feel excluded. It is also the case that the Old Testament as a whole reflects more than one tradition about the meaning of God's choice of Israel and the nature of Israel's role. Along with Genesis, other texts such as Jonah, Ruth and the later chapters of Isaiah reflect a relatively open tradition, in which God's sights are set on all peoples. These texts stand in tension, to some degree, with others such as Joshua, Ezra and Nehemiah, which reflect a tradition that is focused more exclusively on Israel. In its earliest days the Church also had to struggle with tensions around these same traditions, especially in relation to the question whether non-Jews ought to be admitted. Eventually the more open, inclusive tradition held the day in Christianity, so that we know that the new life won for us through Christ's death is won for all of us, Jews and Gentiles alike.

A further aspect about which we should take care is a tendency among some Christians to identify Abraham and his descendants with the modern State of Israel. 'The Jews' and 'the State of Israel' are not the same thing, even though there are important overlaps. Nothing in this book should be taken to suggest that we ought to be uncritical supporters of modern-day Israel, especially in regard to its relationships with near neighbours. If anything, Abraham's story in Genesis ought to cause us to ask questions about these matters. Even though Genesis highlights God's choice of Abraham, and then his choice of Isaac over Ishmael (and so on, over the generations), it also highlights the common origins of Jewish, Christian and Muslim peoples. All are descended from the one family, Genesis reminds us, and from the one ancestor, Abraham.

Journey's end?

Over the course of this book we have seen Abraham undertake a significant journey. At the beginning he set out into the unknown, with an unknown God. By the end of the journey he had become the person God chose him to be – a true patriarch, whose faith and obedience had consequences for everybody around him. All along the way Abraham struggled with a problem, a gap or longing in his life. Abraham wanted a son to be his heir. What he wanted was impossible! Both Abraham and Sarah were old, and Sarah was barren. But God was on their side. With God's help, Abraham came to have faith that he would have an heir, and that his heir would be his own flesh and blood. One by one the early candidates, Lot and Eliezer, were ruled out (Genesis 13.11; 15.4). Abraham and Sarah used their initiative and got themselves a son with the help of Sarah's maid, but in due course Ishmael was ruled out also (Genesis 17.18–22). When Isaac was born, flesh and blood to both of them, their problem seemed, finally, to have been solved. But God stepped in and tested Abraham by asking him to sacrifice Isaac (Genesis 22.2). As we've seen, Abraham passed the test, without actually taking Isaac's life.

But Abraham had other struggles also, and also other strengths. The whole way along the journey Abraham struggled with his faith in the God who had chosen him so unexpectedly. He found it difficult to believe that God would keep his promises. More than once his worries about his own safety caused him to put Sarah directly in harm's way (Genesis 12.10–20; 20.1–18). When God promised them that he would give them a son, Isaac, both Sarah and Abraham responded with laughter, and Abraham seemed primarily concerned with the fate of Ishmael (Genesis 17.15–22;18.12). At the same time as all of those struggles, Abraham appeared to grow in his responsibilities to those around him and in his relationship with God. He offered hospitality to the stranger, even when he was unable to know that the stranger was God (Genesis 18.1–8). He intervened and interceded on behalf of peoples who were not members of his own family, such as the people of Sodom (Genesis 18.22–33) and of Gerar (Genesis 20.7). Finally, when God asked of Abraham the ultimate sacrifice, the lives of his two sons, Abraham obeyed him without question (Genesis 21 and 22).

Often as Christians we tend to lionize Abraham and put him on some kind of a pedestal as a hero of faith. Partly that is connected with the way he is portrayed in the New Testament. As we've followed him and his story in Genesis, however, we've seen that he is a more flawed, or human, character than we often allow. His record is mixed, and he struggled with the kinds of things that we also struggle with. That actually makes him a more helpful model, or companion, for us than he would be as an uncomplicated hero of faith. He struggles and fails and succeeds in the same kind of ways as we do. This aspect of Abraham's character also made him a helpful model, or companion, for the Israelites as they returned from exile in Babylon to find a homeland that didn't fit their expectations. He was a patriarch who came from outside, as they did, who struggled both with his behaviour and with his belief in the reliability of God's promises, as they did, who worried about his legacy, as they did, and who finally proved himself as God's chosen one, as they aspired to do.

All the way through this book I have encouraged you to 'read' your own story in tandem with Abraham's story, as I've also read my own story. I have talked of your story, and mine, as journeys that reflect some of the aspects of Abraham's own journey. I have confidence that along the way you will have found aspects of Abraham's character, and of his story, that resonate with your own. I also hope that, in these final chapters in particular, you have also found aspects that resonate with the great Holy Week and Easter journey – Christ's journey to Jerusalem, to choosing the cross and finally to resurrection. What kind of a companion has Abraham been to you, and on what kind of a journey has he accompanied you? You should now be in a position to stand back and to see something of the shape of the journey you have travelled. It will not necessarily be the case that you have reached the end of this particular journey, even if you can already see the new Easter life to which it has given birth. You may be embarked on a much longer, more arduous journey. Perhaps a journey that looked relatively small and self-contained at the beginning has revealed itself to be more complicated than you had realized. Or perhaps, like me, you have discovered that a long journey which seemed to have been reaching an end point was really only beginning. Whichever is the case for you, Abraham is still there to be a companion and fellow-journeyer with you.

And so it remains only for me to wish you well and God-speed on the journey that you are travelling. I pray that your faith will guide you along the harder places in the road, and that new, Easter, life is waiting for you along the way. May you be granted grace and strength to walk the way of Abraham when the going is tough, and may Jesus Christ always be your guide, so that you might find joy through pain, hope through despair and new life through death. Finally, my friend, I wish you *shalom*.

Questions for reflection

For individuals

1 Looking back, can you see where your journey has taken you? Are you nearing an end-point?
2 What new life are you aware of in your own life? Have there been deaths you have needed to die in order to find it?
3 Which particular aspects of Abraham's journey have you found to be the most helpful to you?

For groups

1 Where do you find evidence of new life in Genesis 26? Who is that life *for*?
2 Can Abraham be a point of focus for inter-religious dialogue and friendship between Jews, Christians and Muslims? Which particular aspects of his story might be helpful here?
3 In what ways might this journey with Abraham help you to talk with other Christians about their journeys of faith?

Further recommended reading

N.B. Some of these books, book chapters and articles are written at a more academic level than others. The more demanding items are marked with *.

Introduction to the Old Testament

Lawrence Boadt   *Reading the Old Testament: An introduction* (New York: Paulist, 1984).

Diana V. Edelman, Philip R. Davies, Christophe Nihan, Thomas Römer   *Opening the Books of Moses* (Sheffield: Equinox, 2012).

Introduction to Genesis

*David M. Carr   *Reading the Fractures of Genesis: Historical and literary approaches* (Louisville: Westminster John Knox, 1996).

R.W.L. Moberly   'Genesis 12–50' in John W. Rogerson, R.W.L. Moberly and William Johnstone, *Genesis and Exodus* (Sheffield: Sheffield, 2001), 100–72.

*R.W.L. Moberly   *The Theology of the Book of Genesis* (Cambridge and New York: Cambridge University Press, 2009).

Reading Genesis in the context of the Persian period

Joseph Blenkinsopp   *Abraham: The story of a life* (Grand Rapids: Eerdmans, 2015).

*Mark G. Brett   *Genesis: Procreation and the politics of identity* (London: Routledge, 2000).

1 The call: Genesis 12.1–18

Norman C. Habel   *The Land is Mine: Six biblical land ideologies* (Minneapolis: Fortress, 1995), 115–33.

2 The promise: Genesis 15

*Ronald Clements   *Abraham and David: Genesis 15 and its meaning for Israelite tradition* (London: SCM, 1967).

*Diana Lipton   *Revisions of the Night: Politics and promises in the patriarchal dreams of Genesis* (Sheffield: Sheffield Academic, 1999).

3 The visitors: Genesis 18.1–15

Megan Warner   'Keeping the way of YHWH: righteousness and justice in Genesis 18—19' in Diana Lipton (ed.), *Universalism and Particularism at Sodom and Gomorrah: Essays in memory of Ron Pirson* (Atlanta: Society of Biblical Literature, 2012), 113–28 (and see also the other essays in this collection).

4 The 'other': Genesis 21.1–21

Mark G. Brett   *Decolonizing God: The Bible in the tides of empire* (Sheffield: Sheffield Phoenix, 2008), 112–31.

*Joel Kaminsky   *Yet I Loved Jacob: Reclaiming the biblical concept of election* (Nashville: Abingdon, 2007).

5 The choice: Genesis 22.1–19

*Jon D. Levenson   *The Death and Resurrection of the Beloved Son* (New Haven; London: Yale, 1993).

*R.W.L. Moberly   *The Bible, Theology and Faith: A study of Abraham and Jesus* (Cambridge: Cambridge University, 2000).

6 The legacy: Genesis 26

*George G. Nicol   'The narrative structure and interpretation of Genesis XXVI, 1–33', *Vetus Testamentum* 46 (1996), 339–60.

Printed in Great Britain
by Amazon